Writing Workbook

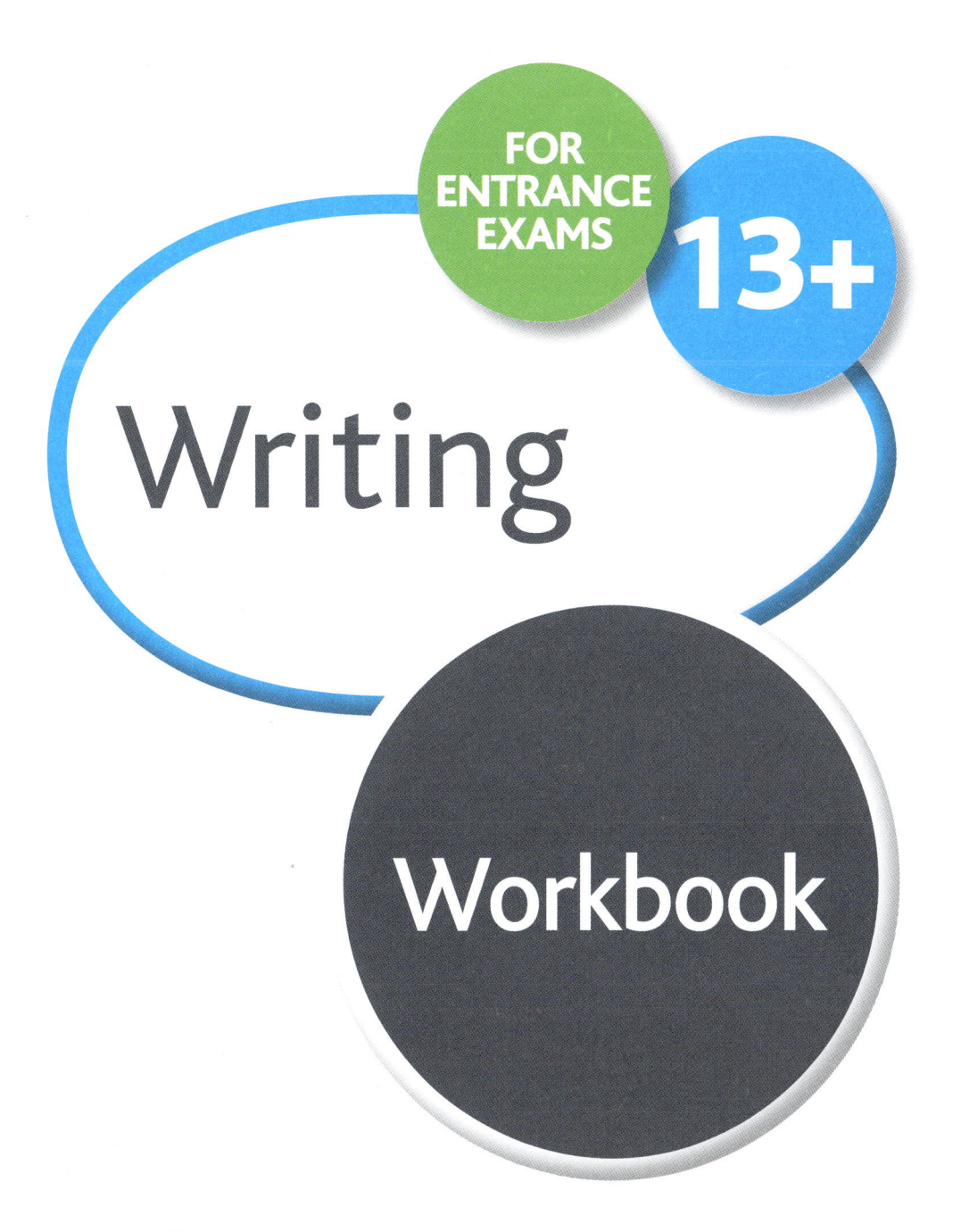

FOR ENTRANCE EXAMS 13+

Victoria Burrill

GALORE PARK
AN HACHETTE UK COMPANY

About the author

Victoria Burrill is Head of English at Newton Prep school in Battersea, London. She teaches Years 5 to 8, preparing children for pre-tests and entrance exams for London Day Schools at both 11+ and 13+ and Common Entrance at 13+. She has written for both Rising Stars and Galore Park for the last four years and her catalogue includes the English for the More Able series, 11+ Practice Papers and Revision Guide and the Galore Park English textbook series for Years 3 to 6. Her particular passion is to instil a love of literature in her students and she plans her lessons around whole novels, using them to teach key skills and to evoke a love of a good story.

Acknowledgements

Every effort has been made to trace all copyright holders, but if any have been inadvertently overlooked, the Publishers will be pleased to make the necessary arrangements at the first opportunity.

Hachette UK's policy is to use papers that are natural, renewable and recyclable products and made from wood grown in sustainable forests. The logging and manufacturing processes are expected to conform to the environmental regulations of the country of origin.

Orders: **Teachers** please contact Bookpoint Ltd, 130 Park Drive, Milton Park, Abingdon, Oxon OX14 4SE. Telephone: (44) 01235 400555. Email primary@bookpoint.co.uk. Lines are open from 9 a.m. to 5 p.m., Monday to Saturday, with a 24-hour message answering service.

Parents, **Tutors** please call: 020 3122 6405 (Monday to Friday, 9:30 a.m. to 4.30 p.m.).
Email: parentenquiries@galorepark.co.uk

Visit our website at www.galorepark.co.uk for details of other revision guides for Common Entrance, examination papers and Galore Park publications.

ISBN: 978 1 5104 2980 2

© Victoria Burrill 2018

First published in 2018 by
Hodder and Stoughton Limited,
An Hachette UK Company
Carmelite House
50 Victoria Embankment
London
EC4Y 0DZ

www.galorepark.co.uk

Impression number   10 9 8 7 6 5 4 3 2 1

Year   2022 2021 2020 2019 2018

All rights reserved. Apart from any use permitted under UK copyright law, no part of this publication may be reproduced or transmitted in any form or by any means, electronic or mechanical, including photocopying and recording, or held within any information storage and retrieval system, without permission in writing from the publisher or under licence from the Copyright Licensing Agency Limited. Further details of such licences (for reprographic reproduction) may be obtained from the Copyright Licensing Agency Limited, www.cla.co.uk

Illustrations by Aptara Inc.

Typeset in India

Printed in India

A catalogue record for this title is available from the British Library.

Contents

- Introduction — 4
- Planning for creative writing — 6
- Planning effective short stories — 8
- Circular planning — 10
- Using different narrative perspectives — 12
- Writing a vignette — 14
- Describing characters — 16
- Sustaining mood — 18
- Building tension — 20
- Structuring descriptions — 22
- Describing settings — 24
- Describing characters — 26
- Structuring a literary essay — 28
- Writing about books — 30
- Using formal language — 32
- Linking ideas together — 34
- Features of non-fiction texts — 36
- Planning to inform, explain and advise — 38
- Writing to inform — 40
- Writing about your personal experience — 42
- Writing to explain — 44
- Writing to advise — 46
- Planning to argue or persuade — 48
- Writing to argue — 50
- Writing to persuade — 54
- Example exam questions — 58
- Topics to be aware of and explore — 60
- Answers (pull-out middle section) — A1

Introduction

Reinforcing and practising writing skills

The aim of this workbook is to offer you an opportunity to consolidate and revise the key building blocks of good writing. Rather than merely working through a string of exam practice tasks, you will tackle the individual elements of effective writing in a number of genres.

To be well prepared for a range of 13+ writing assessments you will need to be comfortable writing in the following genres:

- Narrative – short story writing
- Descriptive – describing settings, characters and events without a clear narrative plot
- Literary essay – writing about a book you have read
- Explaining – providing detailed information about a particular topic, including how something works or happens
- Informing – giving the reader information about something without any bias (which might include telling them about a personal experience)
- Advising – sharing your knowledge and experience with the reader in the form of guidance and suggestions
- Arguing – presenting one or both sides of an argument
- Persuading – convincing the reader to do something or believe something

In addition, you will need to be familiar with writing in different forms such as letters, articles, essays and speeches.

The foundations of these different writing styles are very similar and are summarised in this diagram:

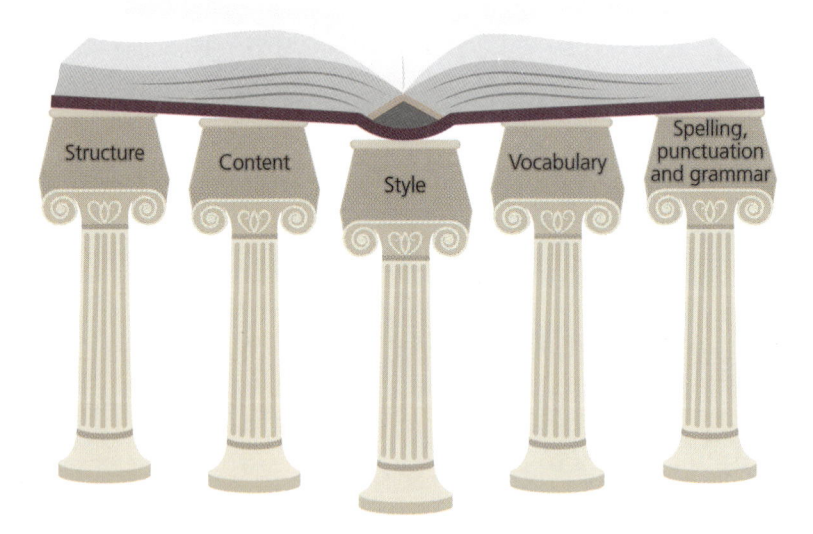

Structure covers aspects of writing that hold the text together. This might be the order of the writing, how information is grouped together in paragraphs or the timeline of a story. This workbook offers advice on how to create an effective structure and how to experiment with different structures for effect. You will also find many planning tasks which are key for practising the structural aspect of writing.

Content is what you actually write about, which might be the plot for a story, the reasons and key points in an argument or the setting in a description. Practising generating content for different text types is vital in preparing for assessment. The more ideas you have already thought through, planned and written about, the easier it will be to write in the exam.

Style encompasses all of the features of a text that are used specifically to fit the purpose, tone or audience. This workbook explores the stylistic features of different text types to help you produce them more effectively. It also covers the use of figurative language for description and technical vocabulary in informative writing. Style also means the use of grammar for effect, such as building tension, and you will also practise this through the tasks.

Vocabulary is more straightforward. It involves the understanding and careful choice of the words you use in your compositions. Carefully selected words have more impact and make an impression on the reader. This workbook offers opportunities to practise these skills and you may choose to develop this element of your writing further in the *13+ Vocabulary Workbook*.

Spelling, punctuation and grammar are concerned with the technical accuracy of writing. Be mindful of these skills as you work through the workbook and identify any aspects of spelling, punctuation or grammar that you need to revise.

How to use this book

This workbook is designed to be used flexibly. You could work through each chapter in turn, or choose to focus on areas you are least confident with first. Each chapter offers three structured tasks: **Try it out**, **Test yourself** and **Extend your skills**:

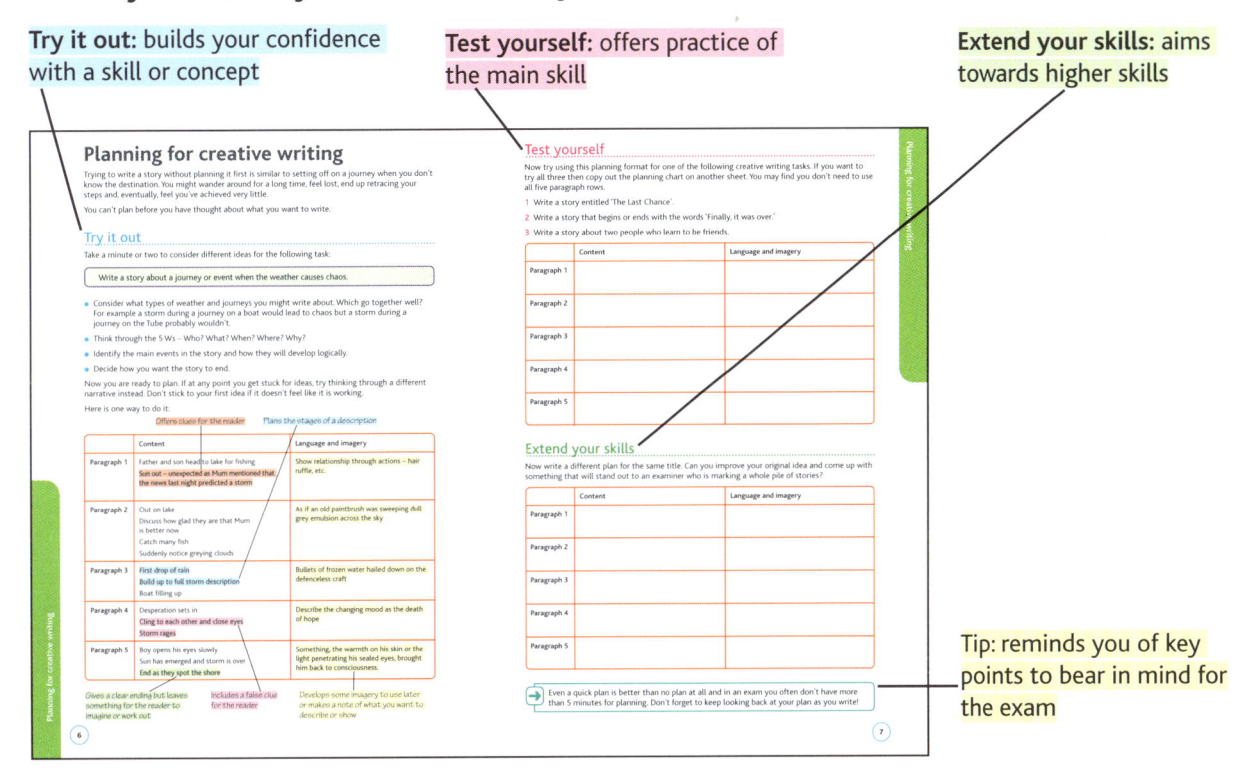

Try it out: builds your confidence with a skill or concept

Test yourself: offers practice of the main skill

Extend your skills: aims towards higher skills

Tip: reminds you of key points to bear in mind for the exam

After completing each chapter, use the Answers section to assess your work, making improvements based on the advice given. You could ask an adult to help you with this. At the back of the workbook you will find example exam-style questions, which you might choose to tackle separately. You will also find an area to make research notes on common topics which are found in exam papers, in particular ISEB papers (see page 60). Completing these should boost your confidence in writing about these subjects.

Marking your work

Some tasks in this workbook have a number indicating marks next to them. This means that there is guidance in the Answers section to help you mark your responses. Marks are given for tasks that are similar to exam questions and/or require you to write a complete piece of text.

Tasks without marks are those that are helping you to practise part of a task or to work on a skill. They represent a part of an exam question or a preparation activity for an exam question.

Planning for creative writing

Trying to write a story without planning it first is similar to setting off on a journey when you don't know the destination. You might wander around for a long time, feel lost, end up retracing your steps and, eventually, feel you've achieved very little.

You can't plan before you have thought about what you want to write.

Try it out

Take a minute or two to consider different ideas for the following task:

> Write a story about a journey or event when the weather causes chaos.

- Consider what types of weather and journeys you might write about. Which go together well? For example a storm during a journey on a boat would lead to chaos but a storm during a journey on the Tube probably wouldn't.
- Think through the 5 Ws – Who? What? When? Where? Why?
- Identify the main events in the story and how they will develop logically.
- Decide how you want the story to end.

Now you are ready to plan. If at any point you get stuck for ideas, try thinking through a different narrative instead. Don't stick to your first idea if it doesn't feel like it is working.

Here is one way to do it:

Offers clues for the reader — *Plans the stages of a description*

	Content	Language and imagery
Paragraph 1	Father and son head to lake for fishing. Sun out – unexpected as Mum mentioned that the news last night predicted a storm	Show relationship through actions – hair ruffle, etc.
Paragraph 2	Out on lake. Discuss how glad they are that Mum is better now. Catch many fish. Suddenly notice greying clouds	As if an old paintbrush was sweeping dull grey emulsion across the sky
Paragraph 3	First drop of rain. Build up to full storm description. Boat filling up	Bullets of frozen water hailed down on the defenceless craft
Paragraph 4	Desperation sets in. Cling to each other and close eyes. Storm rages	Describe the changing mood as the death of hope
Paragraph 5	Boy opens his eyes slowly. Sun has emerged and storm is over. End as they spot the shore	Something, the warmth on his skin or the light penetrating his sealed eyes, brought him back to consciousness.

Gives a clear ending but leaves something for the reader to imagine or work out — *Includes a false clue for the reader* — *Develops some imagery to use later or makes a note of what you want to describe or show*

Test yourself

Now try using this planning format for one of the following creative writing tasks. If you want to try all three then copy out the planning chart on another sheet. You may find you don't need to use all five paragraph rows.

1. Write a story entitled 'The Last Chance'.
2. Write a story that begins or ends with the words 'Finally, it was over.'
3. Write a story about two people who learn to be friends.

	Content	Language and imagery
Paragraph 1		
Paragraph 2		
Paragraph 3		
Paragraph 4		
Paragraph 5		

Extend your skills

Now write a different plan for the same title. Can you improve your original idea and come up with something that will stand out to an examiner who is marking a whole pile of stories?

	Content	Language and imagery
Paragraph 1		
Paragraph 2		
Paragraph 3		
Paragraph 4		
Paragraph 5		

→ Even a quick plan is better than no plan at all and in an exam you often don't have more than 5 minutes for planning. Don't forget to keep looking back at your plan as you write!

Planning effective short stories

In an exam, if you are asked to write a story, it has to be short as you will only have around 40 minutes to write it. However, it can be difficult to make a story gripping and memorable in this short period of time.

Here are some tips for structuring a story that will pack a punch in only a couple of pages:

- Get straight into the action.
  - For example, if your story is about a terrible storm at sea, you need to begin the tale as the grey clouds start to fill the sky, not when the boat sets out from the dock.
- Description is important but include it as you go along, rather than having a long build-up at the start, for example:
  - As Lorna scanned the horizon, she noticed a bank of thick, ash-coloured cloud filling the air above her. The once courageous and fearless Captain Lorna now flinched at the first drop of rain on her skin. She shrank into the cabin to consult her map.

  This description tells us plenty about the character and the setting while also moving the story forward.
- Don't feel that you always need to explain the end of your story. You can leave the reader to work it out, for example:
  - As she saw the final lightning bolt she knew this was her last chance so she swam for her life.

  You don't always have to tell the reader what happened next. Readers like to think for themselves.

It is important to incorporate these ideas into your plan so that you don't end up writing too much introduction or build-up and then running out of time for the exciting action.

Try it out

Finish off the first paragraph of the story about Lorna and the storm that has been introduced above. Remember, the story begins like this:

> As Lorna scanned the horizon, she noticed a bank of thick, ash-coloured cloud filling the air above her. The once courageous and fearless Captain Lorna now flinched at the first drop of rain on her skin. She shrank into the cabin to consult her map.

Use the tips in the bullet points above to help you.

_____

_____

_____

_____

_____

_____

_____

Test yourself

Use the planning chart below (like the one on page 6) to plan a short story in which the action begins straight away in the first paragraph. Your plan should be for one of the following:

- A story about a frightening accident
- A story with the title 'Avalanche'
- A story that ends in disaster.

	Content	Language and imagery
Paragraph 1		
Paragraph 2		
Paragraph 3		
Paragraph 4		
Paragraph 5		

Extend your skills

Plan a short story where the ending is left completely open to interpretation by the reader. The key is to leave the reader enough clues so that they have a good idea of what happens at the end but not so many that they are sure.

_____
_____
_____
_____
_____
_____
_____
_____
_____

Circular planning

In order to make a short story feel complete, you may choose to use a circular structure. This means that your story begins and ends in the same place or time, giving a sense of wholeness for the reader.

This might involve using a flashback to show the character at an earlier point in time. Have a look at the example plan below.

> Write a story that begins with the words 'As she sat gazing out at the garden, she knew things were about to change.'

	Content	Language and imagery
Paragraph 1	Old lady thinks back to when she moved into the house with her new husband Remembers the children being born	
Paragraph 2	Describes happy times with family and friends Children move away Hint at her husband getting ill	
Paragraph 3	Suggestion (not obvious) that her husband passed away She stares out at the now overgrown garden for the last time before moving away	

The story is circular as the old lady begins and ends in the same place (and at the same time). It jumps back in time to fill in the narrative gaps.

In paragraph 1, be sure to indicate to the reader that a flashback is happening – otherwise it can be confusing. To help signal this, use phrases such as:

- She cast her mind back to …
- Memories flooded back to her of …
- She remembered …

> This structure often works well when you are given the first line of the story in an exam. Use the rest of your story to explain the first line by using the flashback technique.

Try it out

Try writing the first paragraph of the story that has been planned above. Think about how you will signpost for the reader that there is a flashback coming. Don't forget that the question requires you to begin with a particular sentence.

_____

_____

_____

_____

Test yourself

Plan a story for each of the following tasks, using a circular structure.

1 Write a story that begins with the words, 'As he picked up the letter, he could feel tears welling up.'

2 Write a story entitled 'The Bully'.

3 Write a story entitled 'Last Chance'.

First sentence	As he picked up the letter, he could feel tears welling up.
Paragraph 1	
Paragraph 2	
Paragraph 3	

Title	The Bully
Paragraph 1	
Paragraph 2	
Paragraph 3	

Title	Last Chance
Paragraph 1	
Paragraph 2	
Paragraph 3	

Extend your skills

Try planning a story, on a separate sheet of paper, where the circular structure extends to using the exact same words at the beginning and end. You might also try to begin and end with a slight variation on a sentence.

For example you could write a story about the bully which begins, 'She was certain that things could only get worse', but ends with 'She was certain things could only get better'.

Using different narrative perspectives

Many narratives are written in the third person (using he, she, it or they). These tend to have a neutral perspective with the narrator being somebody who is not part of the story. Other narratives are told in the first person (using I or we), usually by the main character, giving a deeper insight into the main character's feelings and reactions to events. Both of these perspectives are effective, but in some writing tasks it can add interest to choose a completely different perspective.

There are a few things to consider when choosing a viewpoint from which to write:

- What is the effect on the reader? Will it make it more interesting or will it just be confusing? For example writing a description of a garden from the perspective of a bee would intrigue the reader as they would have to work out whose voice was being heard.
- Are you doing it for a reason? Your choice should add something to the story, for example mystery or detail about the character.
- Will you make it clear at some stage from which viewpoint you are writing? Depending on the plot, this might happen early on or only very late.

Here are some ideas:

- In a story with a chase, write from the viewpoint of the chaser, not the chased.
- Retell a familiar story from the point of view of the villain – perhaps they aren't so bad after all, just misunderstood?
- Consider presenting your story as if it is one thing but then revealing that the viewpoint is different, for example what seems to be people caught in a storm is slowly revealed to be spiders being washed down the plughole in the bath!

Try it out

Think of your favourite books, stories and films. Work out from whose perspective the story is told. Now consider which other perspectives might be interesting to explore. Complete the table below with your ideas for changing perspective. One example has been provided for you.

Story	Original perspective	New perspective	Rationale for change
The Wizard of Oz	Third person	First person – Wicked Witch of the West	To show the witch and Dorothy in a new light

Test yourself

Choose one of the following ideas and try to write the first paragraph from the given point of view. Don't give it away too quickly – try to drop clues for the reader to begin to work it out. They can be subtle at first and then more obvious.

- Retell *The Three Little Pigs* from the wolf's perspective. Aim to make him sound innocent and misunderstood.
- Write a description of an animal being hunted from the point of view of the prey. Make sure it isn't clear right away who is speaking.
- Write about the first day at a new school, as a teacher. You might be able to trick the reader into thinking it is a student at first and only reveal the truth later.

_____
_____
_____
_____
_____
_____
_____
_____
_____ [10 marks]

Extend your skills

On a separate sheet of paper, plan your own story or description based on one of these titles, using an unusual perspective. Then write the first paragraph of your story or description below.

- Below the surface
- Morning rain
- Into the dark

_____
_____
_____
_____
_____
_____
_____
_____

Writing a vignette

In an exam, you generally won't have more than 45 minutes to plan and write your piece of creative writing. For this reason, a useful style of writing to master is the vignette – a short scene focusing on one moment or one character which gives the reader a clear impression about it. It isn't a full story, but the inclusion of a character makes it more than just a description.

Below is the beginning of a vignette about the moment two people met for the first time. It was written in response to the following:

> Write a composition entitled 'Reunited'.

> There was a second when she couldn't quite make him out. The mist was hanging like smoke in the air and his silhouette was barely visible through the mire. As the fog dispersed, her heart began to thump deafeningly in her chest. It had been months that had felt like years since they had last laid eyes on each other. Would he recognise her? Would she feel the same? The haze thinned further and her eyes began to focus on the figure before her. His broad shoulders, the heavy duffel bag slung weightily over his back and finally the glint of his eyes, the hue of melted chocolate.

In this extract, we are introduced to two people who clearly have had a past relationship and have been parted for some reason. So there is some anxiety and some excitement. Emotions are an important part of a vignette about character.

To write a vignette successfully:

- Begin with a clear idea of what you want to reveal about your character(s).
- Don't give too much away too quickly.
- Remember it's just a snapshot – like one scene in a film.
- Focus on the characters' emotions, not the plot.
- At the end, leave the reader to work out what happens next.

> → Vignettes work very well when you can identify a clear emotion that you want to express. Look carefully at task titles to see if they can be interpreted emotionally.

Try it out

Complete the vignette started above.

- Decide what you want the characters to reveal about their relationship – you could explore why they had been apart or why they were so nervous about seeing each other again.
- Think about how to show this through their actions.
- Avoid finishing with a cliché, such as walking off into the sunset. End your piece so that it leaves the reader thinking.

_____

_____

_____

_____

Test yourself

Choose one of the following titles. Then plan and write a vignette in response to the task.

- Hated
- On the edge
- Off the rails
- Blue skies

_____

_____

_____

_____

_____

_____

_____

_____ [10 marks]

Extend your skills

Try writing a vignette which is free of character and evokes the feelings or mood of an object or a setting. Think about how you will express the emotion without a human character. Below is a short example in response to the following task:

> Write a piece entitled 'Delicious'.

The heat from the kitchen was like a magnet. Warm steam seeped through the cracks in the door, comforting aromas tickled the air and suffused the space they inhabited. With each delicious waft of heat came a different scent. The sharp stab of chilli. The comforting pillow of baking bread. The shrill alarm of strong coffee. The all-encompassing and suffocating scents that traversed time and space. Memories of smells. Memories of food. But moreover, memories of life.

Now write your own piece called 'Delicious'.

_____

_____

_____

_____

_____

_____

_____ [10 marks]

Describing characters

Think about the characters you engaged with in the books you have most enjoyed. In many instances, the reason we persevere with books is that we care about the characters; something makes us empathise with them and want to see them succeed or, in the case of popular villainous characters, to witness their downfall.

So, how can you incorporate this idea of engagement into your own writing?

You might choose to create your characters in such a way that the reader feels empathy for them. Some ideas include:

- Paint them as the underdog – someone who never gets a break or any luck.
- Refer briefly to a sad or unfortunate past life event – an illness or bereavement perhaps.
- Your character might be the victim of bullying – whether they are an adult or a child.
- Depending on the length of your story, your character might suffer a setback, injury or partial defeat and then need to fight harder to succeed.

All of these factors will help the reader to care about what happens to your character.

You might design your character so that the reader really wishes and urges them to succeed, for example:

- Make your character very principled or highly moral.
- Describe them as being on a mission to achieve something important.
- Place them in a situation that the reader can identify with – consider your audience and what they might recognise about themselves in your character.

Here is an example:

> As the sound of gunfire grew ever closer, Jake had a momentary flashback to his fifth birthday. The candles, the presents, the laughter … and the absence of his father. That glimpse of the past spurred him on, emboldened him for the fight he knew was imminent. He would do this for his father: he would make him proud.

Try it out

Write a short piece, similar to the one above, which gives your reader a reason to care about your character. Use one of the following ideas:

- A character who is trying to right an injustice
- A character who suffered a trauma earlier in his or her life
- A character who has a special power or gift.

_____

_____

_____

_____

_____

Test yourself

Create a character for each of the following scenarios. Focus on including small details to encourage the reader to empathise with and root for them as they continue reading your story.

1 Describe a character who is going to overcome bullying at school.

_____
_____
_____
_____
_____
_____
_____

2 Describe a character who has to face a challenge to save his or her family.

_____
_____
_____
_____
_____
_____
_____

3 Describe a character who goes on a physically challenging journey to seek revenge.

_____
_____
_____
_____
_____
_____
_____ [10 marks]

Extend your skills

Take your favourite character from above. Then, on a separate sheet of paper, plan and write a short story with this character as the protagonist. Design the story so that you can drop in references to the character's background throughout the narrative, increasing the reader's feelings of empathy as they read on, for example if you choose the character who is seeking revenge, use flashbacks or memories to remind the reader of his or her motives. [10 marks]

Sustaining mood

The best stories and descriptions enable the reader to feel like they are living the action, like they are right there as part of the story. In order to do this, you need to build and, more importantly, continue a mood.

Read this example:

> This part of the forest was darker than the others. The trees reached over Michael's head, suffocating any mournful rays of light from the waning moon. The air hung cold around him and chilled him to the very marrow of his bones. Decaying leaves festered under his feet and the crackle of the dead foliage, clutching onto the branches for dear life, reminded him that this was a place steeped in lifelessness. A forest graveyard where only the spirits of the deceased haunted the night.

The highlighted words all have negative and deathly connotations or ideas and this helps to sustain the creepy and frightening mood.

By continually choosing words with appropriate connotations, you can sustain the mood for the reader. Imagine if the following sentences came next:

> The wind picked up and whistled through the trees like a mellifluous choir. The tendrils of the wind tickled his skin.

Now the connotations have changed to be more positive (for example whistled, mellifluous, choir, tickled) and the sombre mood has been broken.

→ Use imagery to help sustain the mood as well as to envisage your scene, for example similes (such as 'like a mellifluous choir') and personification ('the wind tickled his skin'), as well as metaphors.

Try it out

You are going to describe the same setting but with two opposite moods.

1 First, imagine a mountaintop on a bright sunny day. You have reached the top, the sky is cloudless and blue and you are feeling triumphant after your climb.

2 Next imagine the same mountaintop in the midst of a terrifying snowstorm.

In the table below, list some adjectives and verbs you might use for the two different scenarios.

	Triumphant climb	Dangerous blizzard
Verbs		
Adjectives		

Test yourself

Write one of these setting descriptions, ensuring you sustain the mood throughout the paragraph. Choose your words and imagery carefully to build up a sense of the atmosphere for the reader.

- Describe an abandoned hospital.
- Describe a bustling party.
- Describe a funeral.

_____
_____
_____
_____
_____
_____
_____
_____
_____ [10 marks]

Extend your skills

Another good way to sustain mood is to use an extended metaphor to describe a place or a feeling. This involves choosing a theme for your imagery and continuing this throughout a piece of writing, for example you might describe a raging fire like a disease, making use of vocabulary related to the idea of a disease.

> The fiery plague contaminated the forest with its contagious touch. It blistered everything it touched, drew the life from its victims and infected the vulnerable earth with its heat.

Now, either continue this description of a fire or devise your own extended metaphor to describe a fire.

_____
_____
_____
_____
_____
_____
_____
_____ [10 marks]

Building tension

In a narrative, tension is the anticipation that something is going to happen. It evokes an emotion: fear, excitement, anxiety, to name but a few. The tension is only broken when the unknown becomes known to the reader. While the technique works well in the horror or mystery genres, it is equally applicable to other types of text. Think of the star-crossed lovers who may not end up together or the adventurer on the high seas who may just reach land before the storm.

Tension helps the reader to empathise with the character and to feel part of the story. There are a number of ways to achieve it:

- Don't give everything away too soon – leave the reader with questions.
- At the start of a story, use pronouns (he, she, it) without revealing who or what they are.
- Occasionally use short sentences (or paragraphs) to draw attention to sudden events or to highlight a particular emotion.
- Use the 'show not tell' technique to hint at the character's feelings rather than being too obvious.
- Include one or two questions to encourage the reader to wonder about the same things as the characters.
- Input a sense of urgency, such as a deadline or time constraint, on the character.

These are just some of many techniques. Have a look at them in action below:

> Jack knew it was only a matter of time before she caught up with him. She'd been hot on his heels before the last blast. He continued to step carefully through the rubble, desperately trying to still the quivering in his legs. The explosion had muted his senses but his commitment to survival remained strong. He looked around him through the dust, scanning the unfamiliar environment for an exit point. Suddenly a movement. A shadow. Was it her?
>
> He ducked behind an almost obliterated concrete pillar and took a breath. Where next? He didn't have long.

→ Tension is about prompting an emotion in the reader. Try experimenting with using tension in love stories, adventure tales and stories of everyday life.

Try it out

Create a chase scene between two characters – they needn't both be human. Use the techniques described above to build tension. Don't be afraid to withhold crucial details from the reader. This will only draw them further into your story.

_____
_____
_____
_____
_____
_____
_____

Test yourself

Choose one of the following titles and write the first paragraph of a short story, using a range of techniques from the page opposite to build tension.

- The result
- She who dares, wins
- Lost

_____
_____
_____
_____
_____
_____
_____
_____
_____
_____
_____
_____
_____
_____
_____
_____
_____ [10 marks]

Extend your skills

In some short stories, the tension builds but is never completely broken, for example a detective solves a crime but cannot arrest the criminal, so the reader is left wondering if the crimes might continue.

On a separate sheet of paper, plan and write a short story which is rich in tension but which is never fully resolved. Make sure that the story has an ending but do not write a clichéd cliffhanger. [25 marks]

Structuring descriptions

Story structures are often quite simple – beginning, build-up, climax, resolution, ending – as shown in the diagram below. When there is a clear plot, the story often writes itself. However, with a description, the lack of plot or protagonist can be problematic. At their worst, descriptions can be muddled and disorderly.

Although there is not a plot line in a description, it does need some kind of direction so that the reader can feel that they are making some progress. Below are a number of suggestions for how to structure your descriptions in interesting and effective ways.

Settings:

- Morning through to night
- Winter through to summer
- A tour of the place – moving from one area to another
- From low down to high up, for example for a forest
- From beginning to end, for example for a market or sporting event
- Sense by sense – sight, sound, smell, taste and touch (the last two are not always possible, depending on the subject of the description)

Characters:

- From viewing them far away to seeing them up close
- From their feet up to the top of their head or vice versa (this works well when writing about a big character from a small character's perspective or vice versa)
- Sense by sense (sight, sound, smell, taste, touch) – include some metaphorical ideas, for example 'the smell of fear oozed from his skin'

Remember that you decide your structure at the planning stage, so give it some thought before you put your plan down on paper.

Try it out

Plan a setting description of a garden in two different ways. Choose from the ideas above or use your own idea. Make sure your choice of structure adds to what you are trying to tell the reader about the garden, for example if you want to show the way a garden transforms throughout the seasons, use that as your structure.

_____

_____

_____

_____

_____

_____

> → Certain subjects lend themselves more to one structure than another, for example if you want to demonstrate how intimidating a tall character is to a shorter character, incorporate that into your structure.

Test yourself

Write a plan for each of these description tasks. Use a different structure for each one.

- Write a description of a bustling market.

	Content	Language and imagery
Paragraph 1		
Paragraph 2		
Paragraph 3		

- Write a description of an eccentric person.

	Content	Language and imagery
Paragraph 1		
Paragraph 2		
Paragraph 3		

- Write a description of a deserted city.

	Content	Language and imagery
Paragraph 1		
Paragraph 2		
Paragraph 3		

Extend your skills

Now try to incorporate the work you have already done on perspective on page 12 with the idea of structure. Depending on whose voice you are using, you might structure the piece differently, for example a child describing a park might start with the playground and describe it in great detail, whereas an adult might notice the flora and fauna.

Write a description of a familiar place but from a perspective other than your own. You might even choose the perspective of a non-human, for example a garden described from the viewpoint of a bee or bird.

_____

_____

_____

_____

_____

_____

_____ [10 marks]

Describing settings

Creating a range of setting descriptions is a useful exam preparation activity. Once you have planned and written them, bank them in your memory to use or adapt in an exam situation. You may be able to use part of them in a description, or they might be shortened as part of a narrative.

There will be opportunities to adapt them to suit other tasks, for example imagine you have practised describing a desert. You don't need to wait for the task 'Describe a desert.' Here are some other tasks in which you might use elements of what you have practised:

- The Longest Journey – you could write a story set in a desert
- Alone – you could write a description of how it feels to be lost in the desert
- Heavy Work – you could create a story about slaves building the Egyptian pyramids.

When you are developing your descriptions, consider using:

- books you have read and films you have seen based in similar settings
- your own experience and memories
- emotions associated with that type of place
- imagery of the five senses
- precise vocabulary
- similes, metaphors and personification (remember what you learnt about sustaining mood on page 18).

The idea of practising is to offer you a chance to think of ideas, develop imagery and research new vocabulary. This gives you a basis for writing about a similar topic in timed conditions.

→ Remember, never rote learn descriptions or stories. Examiners will spot very quickly if you have pre-prepared a piece of writing and tried to match it to a new task.

Try it out

Complete the left-hand column in the table below with some common settings that you might read or write about. In the right-hand column, add notes about whether you have personal experience of them or experience of them through film or literature.

Setting	Experience from literature/film or personal experience

Test yourself

Fill in the table below with a range of vocabulary for each setting, especially adjectives and verbs, figurative language and other carefully crafted phrases.

Setting	Your ideas for vocabulary
Lake/sea shore	
Desert	
Forest/wood	
Busy urban environment	
Medieval castle	
Futuristic city	
Abandoned/run-down building	
School corridor between lessons	

Extend your skills

Linking your ideas together in full sentences is the next step in creating a description. However, it is easy to fall into the trap of repeatedly using long, complex sentences full of multi-syllabic words and well-developed imagery. Although this may sound sophisticated, it becomes difficult for the reader to wade through.

Choose one of the settings above and write a description in which you vary the sentence length and structure to add interest and alter the pace for the reader. Include at least one one-word sentence.

_____
_____
_____
_____
_____
_____
_____
_____ [10 marks]

Describing characters

Describing characters is key to getting the reader to engage with them. Everything you mention about a character should add to the picture you want the reader to have. Anything that doesn't reveal more about the nature of their character or what their motivations are, can be left out.

Read this example:

> He wore brown trousers, a blue checked shirt and green woolly sweater. His shoes were leather and he carried a rucksack, slung over one shoulder.

In this example, the clothes the man wears don't tell the reader anything about his personality, his background, his circumstances or his feelings. Now read the following:

> His trousers reached only to his bare ankles while his checked shirt was frayed and worn. The fabric poked through the threadbare seams of his jumper. His worn soles scraped on the floor and the overstuffed, stained rucksack weighed him down into a slouch.

In this example, the way the man is dressed suggests that he might be homeless, down on his luck, in poverty or neglected. It is not *what* he wears but the condition of his clothes that shows the reader something.

You can also use this 'show not tell' technique to express the character's traits to the reader. It is far more interesting for the reader to be left to work things out rather than to be bluntly told things.

Read this example, in which the reader is told that the character is happy:

> She was elated; so happy that she was grinning from ear to ear.

Now consider this example:

> Her eyes lit up like fireworks as she threw her arms triumphantly into the air. Her lips felt like they would burst through the sides of her cheeks as they ached from smiling.

Here, the reader can assume that the character is happy and can far better imagine what she is experiencing.

Try it out

Write a short description of a suspicious person. Use the way they are dressed and their facial expressions and actions to show how untrustworthy they are. Aim to write five or six sentences.

_____

_____

_____

_____

_____

_____

Test yourself

It is useful exam preparation to have practised describing a range of character types. Choose one (or more) of the adjectives below and write a paragraph describing a character who fits this description, using the 'show not tell' skills you practised earlier.

- arrogant
- shy
- confused
- enthusiastic
- angry
- frightened
- bored
- vengeful

_____
_____
_____
_____
_____
_____
_____
_____
_____ [10 marks]

→ When you are showing not telling, avoid using the adjective that you want the reader to associate with the character. What you show them in terms of actions, voice, stance, expression, gesture and the reactions of others should be enough for this to be worked out by the reader.

Extend your skills

As you may have seen, in literature characters are not always as they first appear. Try writing a short description of a character who at first glance appears one way but then does, says or shows something that reveals them to be otherwise. You almost want to trick the reader into judging someone by their appearance so that when they realise they are wrong, they will then engage far more with the character.

_____
_____
_____
_____
_____
_____
_____ [10 marks]

Structuring a literary essay

You will often find tasks in the exam on writing about a particular focus in a book you have read or studied. It is important to plan a clear structure for these essays so that you address the question effectively and don't repeat yourself.

Here are some example essay questions:

- Write about a book that made you experience a particular emotion.
- Write about a book you have read that addressed the theme of friendship.
- Write about a book that you would like to read again or would recommend.

The best preparation for these tasks is to read widely across a range of genres. Then, before planning your essay, you should think carefully and select an appropriate book for the task.

Your structure should look something like this:

Introduction
Introduce basic information about the book (title, author, theme, brief outline of the plot). Make it clear, in a general way, how this book links to the question.

Main paragraphs (2 to 3)
In each paragraph, you should write about a different element of the book and how it links to the question topic. Elements include: plot, character, setting, theme, tone, perspective, author's message, language and structure.

Make sure each paragraph has a clear purpose.

For example, for the task 'Write about a book that you would like to read again', the main paragraphs might look like this:

Paragraph 1: a particular character with whom you identify and how he or she relates to a main theme

Paragraph 2: the appeal of the use of language in the book

Paragraph 3: the structure – reread to see how earlier events led to the ending

Conclusion
Sum up the different ways in which the book and your experience of the book link to the question. Express your personal response to the book in relation to the question topic.

Try it out

Think about the books you have read recently. Now look at the three example questions above. Make a list of which books you know well that you could write about for each question. If you are struggling to choose one, you might like to plan a visit to the library.

_____

_____

_____

_____

Test yourself

Try planning a response to one of these essay questions. Remember to make sure that your main paragraphs each make a different and clear point about the book.

- Write about a book that made you laugh.
- 'There is no friend as loyal as a book.' Write about a book that you have read many times and to which you feel very loyal.
- Write about a book that really fired your imagination.

Essay title	
Introduction	
Main paragraph 1	
Main paragraph 2	
Main paragraph 3	
Conclusion	

Extend your skills

The next step in writing a literary essay is to compare and contrast two books. To do this, you need to think about their similarities and differences in terms of plot, characterisation, language, structure, theme and historical or social context.

Look at the following themes and choose two books that share one of them.

> love   conflict   power   friendship   courage   difference   loss   survival   change   growing up

Theme: _____ Book 1: _____ Book 2: _____

On a separate sheet of paper, plan an essay in which you compare how the two books deal with your chosen theme. Then write the first paragraph of your essay below.

_____
_____
_____
_____
_____ [10 marks]

Writing about books

To write well about a novel, you will need to include a number of elements in your writing. Although the focus of the essay will be guided by the question, there are a few essential techniques you can use to make your essay stand out:

Be specific to the text:

- Mention particular characters, for example: The author developed empathy for the character of Bruno by …
- Refer to particular episodes within the narrative, for example: The turning point in the narrative was when …
- If you can remember any quotations, include those too.

Give opinions with evidence:

- Always give a reason why you think something about the text, for example: This episode in the novel was emotionally powerful because of the use of …
- You don't need to memorise quotations but do refer to:
  - techniques used by the author, for example: The author's repeated use of short chapters helps to build up the tension …
  - structure, for example: By writing from a variety of viewpoints, the author enables the reader to see the issue from all angles …
  - characterisation, for example: The author develops Bruno's character via the way he misunderstands adults' intentions and mimics their language inaccurately …
  - atmosphere, for example: Through his use of extended metaphor, the author builds an atmosphere of …

Make comparisons with other texts:

- Compare characters in the book with those from other books, for example: The protagonist reminds the reader of Oliver Twist …
- Compare with books from similar settings, time periods or genres, for example: Similarly to other books set in Victorian London, such as …
- Compare with books by the same author, for example: In contrast to Malorie Blackman's other novels …

Try it out

Choose a book you have read or studied in detail and make notes on each of these topics:

Main character	
Structure	
Writing techniques	
Links to other books	

Test yourself

Write about a book that you found memorable. Describe what was so appealing about it and how the book affected you.

_____

[25 marks]

→ It is advisable to write about a book you have studied at school as you will have analysed it in greater depth than a book you have read independently. Talk to your teacher about this.

Extend your skills

It is often harder to write about a book that you did not enjoy. On a separate sheet of paper, write a paragraph explaining why you didn't enjoy a particular book you have read. [10 marks]

Using formal language

When you are writing essays, and most letters, speeches and articles, you are likely to need to use a formal style of language. (There will be some exceptions as a task may instruct you to write more humorously or informally.) Formal language is used in serious situations and often when writing or speaking to people you do not know well.

There are several elements to writing in a formal style:

- Your writing should sound mature and grown up:
  - Choose longer, more sophisticated words, for example: He endeavoured (tried) to resolve (fix) the predicament (problem).
  - Aim to use a mixture of simple and complex sentences.
- Choose words for their specific meaning rather than using generalisations. Think about exactly what it is you mean:
  - Technology isn't 'getting better'; it is 'improving', 'developing' or 'being upgraded'.
- Choose vocabulary linked to your topic to sound more formal and knowledgeable, for example:
  - We live in a world where millions of gigabytes of data are being transmitted via the internet every day.
- Avoid words and phrases that sound like spoken language:
  - Avoid contractions ('would not' rather than 'wouldn't').
  - Don't use any slang words, for example use 'goodbye' rather than 'see ya'.
  - Avoid starting sentences in a spoken fashion, such as 'So …' or 'Well …'.

> → There is a difference between informal language and slang. You might write an informal letter to a grandparent but you probably wouldn't use these phrases: 'Sorry I can't come to visit but my parents busted me sneaking out to a wicked party.'

Try it out

Rewrite this passage, making it more formal. You don't need to change the content, just the style.

> What's up, buddy? How's it going? It's been ages since we hung out. What have you been up to? My mate and me went to a wicked beach last weekend. The surfing was on point but Mum lost the plot cos we rocked up at home a bit late. She's grounded me but being stuck at home is killing me! I'm gutted I'll miss your party on Friday. Hope it's off the hook.

_____
_____
_____
_____
_____

Answers

Planning for creative writing (page 6)

Try it out

Answers will vary. Ideas may include: a plane journey with terrible turbulence and landing somewhere unusual; a long walk where the fog comes in and people get lost; or a car journey which is interrupted by heavy rain and flooding.

Test yourself

Answers will vary. Plans should clearly relate to the title of the piece of writing. Plots should be simple but well developed. Ideas for vocabulary should be relevant and imaginative.

Extend your skills

Answers will vary. Plans should show creative and relevant interpretations of the title that are significantly different from those in the **Test yourself** section; for example, the 'Finally, it was over' task might start with those words and continue with a flashback.

Planning effective short stories (page 8)

Try it out

Answers will vary. The rest of this opening paragraph should involve some kind of action (for example, the ship gets tossed violently to one side). It should also include ongoing description of the storm.

Test yourself

Plans will vary but might include:
- A story about a frightening accident – an ice-skating accident in which the ice cracks and it is not entirely clear whether or not the skater is rescued.
- A story with the title 'Avalanche' – stories should start with characters already on the mountain as the avalanche should happen early in the story.
- A story that ends in disaster – the cause of the disaster should happen quickly in the story, and outcome of the disaster should be implied but not made too obvious.

Extend your skills

Answers will vary. Stories should be constructed so that two or more outcomes are possible from the start. For example: A parachutist who gets distracted while packing his chute worries about it in the plane but allays his fears, jumps and then enjoys the freefall – the ending should not be given away.

Circular planning (page 10)

Try it out

Answers will vary but should clearly highlight for the reader when a flashback starts and stops, using phrases such as 'She thought back to …' or 'Her thoughts drifted back to when …'

Test yourself

Answers will vary. The story should start and end with the same phrase, in the same place or with the same idea to achieve the circular structure.

Extend your skills

Answers will vary. Ideas might include a character's thought or something they say which is repeated at the start and end, or a general statement (for example 'Sometimes you have to know when to speak up').

Using different narrative perspectives (page 12)

Try it out

Answers will vary. For possible ideas see table at bottom of page.

Test yourself

Answers will vary.

Example answer: *The Three Little Pigs* – Everyone gets hungry, don't they? So, what do they do? Pop to the shops, go to a restaurant? Well, us wolves don't have that luxury. We have to hunt for our food and when it comes pre-packaged in a nice house, that's a real treat.

- 1–3 marks: Written from the new perspective but may be inconsistent. Character doesn't really come across or sounds more like a narrator.
- 4–6 marks: Written from the new perspective but may not be very clear. Shows some elements of the character in the writing.
- 7–10 marks: Writing really shows the character of the perspective being written from. It is empathetic and adds to the picture of that character.

Extend your skills

Answers will vary. Ideas for the three titles might include:
- Below the surface – a story of a sinking ship from the perspective of a whale or other sea creature.
- Morning rain – told from the point of view of a caterpillar or spider getting washed away.
- Into the dark – an animal going into hibernation.

These pieces are likely to be written in the first person.

Story	Original perspective	New perspective	Rationale for change
Star Wars	Third person – the Jedi point of view	First person – Darth Vader	To show whether he is as bad as most think
Snow White	Third person – the princess's point of view	First person – one of the dwarves	To show how he feels about their houseguest

English 13+ Workbook: Writing by Galore Park

Writing a vignette (page 14)

Try it out

Answers will vary but should include the same characters and setting. Nothing too exciting should happen but the reason for the characters' meeting should become at least partly clear.

Test yourself

Answers will vary.

- 1–3 marks: Loosely linked to title. May include too much action for a vignette. May lack descriptive techniques and language.
- 4–6 marks: Linked to the chosen title. Characters partly developed. Includes description and emotion but may lack imagery.
- 7–10 marks: Imaginatively linked to title. Clearly just a short scene but engaging and interesting for the reader. Characters' emotions well developed using descriptive techniques.

Extend your skills

Answers will vary.

- 1–3 marks: Loosely linked to the title 'Delicious'. May include too much action for a vignette. Likely to lack descriptive techniques and language.
- 4–6 marks: Linked to title. Setting partly developed, using some sensory description.
- 7–10 marks: Imaginatively linked to title. Setting very well developed, using descriptive techniques and sensory description to draw out emotion. A snapshot, not full of action.

Describing characters (page 16)

Try it out

Answers will vary. The best responses will refer to the character's defining feature in a subtle way rather than spelling it out.

Example answer for a scenario of someone who suffered a trauma:

As he hobbled slowly across the cold floor of the hospital ward, he could still hear the screeching brakes of the motorcycle coming towards him. The smell of the spilled petrol still lingered in his nostrils and, when he closed his eyes, he could still hear the sirens approaching.

Test yourself

Answers will vary.

- 1–3 marks: Characters are only partially developed with little reference to emotion. Description may refer more to appearance than character, voice, movement or background.
- 4–6 marks: Characters are established but may not be sustained. Reference will be made to why the characters are that way but it might not be done subtly.
- 7–10 marks: Characters are well developed and sustained through relevant detail, in particular using the 'show not tell' technique. Empathy should be clearly evoked in the reader.

Extend your skills

Answers will vary.

- 1–3 marks: Story is not developed around the character; they are just in it.
- 4–6 marks: Story is clearly centred on the character but references to their backstory may be obvious or awkward.
- 7–10 marks: Story structure supports the revealing of the character's backstory, which is integral to the plot.

Sustaining mood (page 18)

Try it out

Answers for verbs and adjectives will vary. Examples include:

	Triumphant climb	Dangerous blizzard
Verbs	glisten, ascend, arise	tower, slash, invade
Adjectives	magnificent, regal, powdery	monolithic, menacing, insurmountable

Test yourself

Answers will vary.

- 1–3 marks: Vocabulary is appropriate but not adventurous and may not all support the mood.
- 4–6 marks: Vocabulary is adventurous but not developed into imagery. It should mostly support the mood but it may not always be sustained.
- 7–10: Vocabulary is adventurous and sophisticated and developed into imagery. The mood is sustained throughout the piece.

Extend your skills

Answers will vary.

- 1–3 marks: Metaphors are used but they are not all linked to one theme.
- 4–6 marks: Some attempt made to link the imagery to the theme but it is not consistent. A single extended metaphor has not quite been achieved.
- 7–10 marks: Extended metaphor is consistent throughout the piece and is appropriate to the theme. It has been chosen so that there are many elements of comparison, most of which have been explored.

Building tension (page 20)

Try it out

Answers will vary. Look for evidence of a variety of the techniques in the bullet list on page 20, especially the occasional use of short sentences for sudden developments or the use of questions to reflect tenseness in the character(s). The tension should be sustained until almost the very end.

Test yourself

Answers will vary.

- 1–3 marks: Some tension is created but it might be quickly broken with too much information. Ellipses may be over relied on.
- 4–6 marks: A range of techniques used. Tension is built but may not be sustained. An ellipsis might be used.
- 7–10 marks: A sense of mystery should be clear from the first sentence. A range of techniques should be used. The ending should invite the reader to keep thinking after they have finished reading. The best examples will not need to use an ellipsis to achieve this.

English 13+ Workbook: Writing by Galore Park

Extend your skills

Answers will vary. The best examples of this type of story tell the reader just enough of what happens so that they can work out the ending without being told. The ending should not be over-explained; that is for the reader to do once they have finished reading.

Example ending: a story about a prison break in which the reader knows the criminal got out of jail but doesn't know if he's ever caught after that. It might end 'And freedom was his … for now.'

The 25 marks available for this question are split as follows:

- Content (/10): Closely linked to title, planned to include tension, idea well developed with detail, characters developed through action or dialogue, ending leaves the reader thinking, reader is largely sure they know what happened but not 100 per cent.
- Vocabulary (/5): Relevant, sophisticated, carefully chosen vocabulary that builds mood and adds to the tension.
- Style (/5): A range of devices for building tension including sentence structures, descriptive techniques, varied sentence openers.
- Spelling and punctuation (/5): Common spellings and some more complex spellings accurate, punctuation accurate, a wide range of punctuation used (including semi-colons, brackets, dashes, and so on).

Structuring descriptions (page 22)

Try it out

Plans will vary and may be structured according to: time of day, time of year, part of the garden, from a range of perspectives. The best plans will use structure to back up content and mood.

Example structure: if the mood is sombre as the garden dies in winter then starting the description in the summer, then autumn, then winter would be best. If the mood is about new life, starting the description in the autumn, then winter and spring would make more sense.

Test yourself

Answers will vary. Structures for these descriptions could include:

- Bustling market: morning through to night or different parts of the market, or from different viewpoints (for example child, shopper, market-stall holder), senses.
- Eccentric person: voice, movement, appearance from shoes up to hair.
- Deserted city: zooming in gradually from far away to up close or focusing on streets, buildings, parks (different parts of the city) or different times of the day.

Extend your skills

Answers will vary.

- 1–3 marks: Description is likely to be in first person but may not clearly show whose perspective. Language may be simple and will not reflect the nature of the speaker.
- 4–6 marks: A clear perspective is given but language choices may not reflect this. Viewpoint may not be sustained throughout.
- 7–10 marks: Language is used to show who the speaker is without overtly stating it. This may be revealed later in the piece. Viewpoint is sustained and carefully chosen for the context.

Describing settings (page 24)

Try it out

Answers will vary.

Test yourself

Answers will vary. Look out for examples of metaphor and simile in the example ideas below.

Setting	Example ideas for vocabulary
Lake/sea shore	Magnetic force of the tide Golden silk beach
Desert	Expanse of emptiness Golden mountains that crumble at your touch
Forest/wood	Guardians of the forest Kaleidoscope of leaves
Busy urban environment	Headlights like the eyes of a prowling jaguar Slick mirrored tarmac snaking through the urban jungle
Medieval castle	Crowned with turrets The jaws of the portcullis snapping at its prey
Futuristic city	Glass buildings like mirrors to the sky Cars floating like gulls then swooping down to their nests
Abandoned/run-down building	Creaking floorboards heralding your arrival Damp air choking you with its mouldy grasp
School corridor between lessons	Cacophony of voices like an untuned orchestra Educational rush hour

Extend your skills

Answers will vary. Example setting description:

Night. The city never sleeps, never rests, never quiets. Even when the moon rises like a beacon in the velvet black sky and when restless children are tucked up in beds like cocoons, the city lives. Dark roads snake through the monolithic buildings. Streetlights flicker like budding flowers, smoke exhales from chimneys like frozen breath, the heart of the city beats to the rhythm of the hustle and bustle. Alive. The city is alive.

- 1–3 marks: Some sentence length variation is included but for no clear effect.
- 4–6 marks: Short sentences are used for emphasis but may not always be effective.
- 7–10 marks: Sentence lengths varied effectively – long sentences used for detailed description or to show a busy or crowded scene or to make a list sound longer. Short sentences used for emphasis, to slow the pace down or used alone as a paragraph.

Describing characters (page 26)

Try it out

Answers will vary. Descriptions may refer to shadowy or dark elements, hidden movements, sneaking around or hushed voices when portraying the suspicious character.

Test yourself

Answers will vary.

- 1–3 marks: Characteristics match given task but may be described in an obvious way. Irrelevant detail may also be included. Adjectives may describe the character too directly rather than hinting at character traits.
- 4–6 marks: Descriptions are chosen to tell more about the character. Attempts at more subtle ways to show character may be used but ideas may be clichéd or not sustained.
- 7–10 marks: Description clearly conveys character and feelings through actions, movement, voice and facial expression. More exact use of precise details. 'Show not tell' is used consistently. Emotion- and personality-related adjectives are avoided.

Extend your skills

Answers will vary.

- 1–3 marks: Real character traits may be given away too quickly. Real character may not emerge clearly. Choices of the two possible sides to the character may not overlap enough to wrong-foot the reader successfully.
- 4–6 marks: Character choices are feasible for the task. Some attempt to convey the misinterpretation is evident but may not be successful.
- 7–10 marks: Character is designed so that they show characteristics which can easily be misconstrued. 'Show not tell' is used and by the end the reader recognises that their first impression was wrong.

Structuring a literary essay (page 28)

Try it out

Answers will vary depending on choice of books.

Test yourself

Answers will vary. Plans should show close adherence to the topic of the question. The book choice should be suitable and a range of discrete points should be made, grouped carefully into paragraphs so that the ideas flow towards a brief conclusion.

Extend your skills

Answers will vary.

- 1–3 marks: First paragraph may go into too many specific details rather than make general comparisons. Comparison may be too simplistic and not touch on theme.
- 4–6 marks: Some general areas of comparison and contrast may be outlined. The theme is identified and related to each book.
- 7–10 marks: The theme of both books is clearly outlined and some reference is made to how it features in each text. A statement about whether they are largely similar or different is also made.

Writing about books (page 30)

Try it out

Answers will vary depending on choice of book.

Test yourself

Answers will vary. The 25 marks available for this question are split as follows:

- Content (/10): Clearly structured with introduction and conclusion, paragraphs that make clear points backed up with evidence, close link to given task, range of appealing aspects of the book touched on.
- Vocabulary (/5): Book-related language, sophisticated and varied vocabulary is used.
- Style (/5): Formal language, evidence of references to other books and imagery, varied sentence structure and length, emotive language or humour may be used.
- Spelling and punctuation (/5): Common spellings and some more complex spellings accurate, punctuation accurate, a wide range of punctuation used (including semi-colons, brackets, dashes, and so on).

Extend your skills

Answers will vary.

- 1–3 marks: Refers to weak aspects about the book but may lack reasons. Simple explanations. More personal responses than comments on quality of the book.
- 4–6 marks: Some reference to techniques used by the author with some personal response. Some explanation of book's weaknesses.
- 7–10 marks: Clear explanation supported by personal views of why the book was not enjoyable, with reference to a range of aspects of the book including language, plot, character, structure.

Using formal language (page 32)

Try it out

Answers will vary. Example answer:

How are you, my friend? Are you well? It has been a very long time since I was last in your company. What has happened in your life since we last met? I went to a wonderful beach with a friend of mine last week. We did some excellent surfing but my mother was very angry when we arrived home after our curfew. I'm not allowed out of the house, but being indoors all day is very frustrating! I am very disappointed that I will miss your party on Friday. I hope you have a wonderful evening.

Test yourself

Answers will vary.

- 1–3 marks: The letter and email are quite similar and do not show a clear difference between formal and informal.
- 4–6 marks: The letter and email are different in tone but the formal letter is not very formal and does not use sophisticated or specific language.
- 7–10 marks: The letter and email are clearly different in tone and the formal language is sophisticated and precise, and words as well as syntax are formal.

Extend your skills

Answers will vary.

- 1–3 marks: Voices of the two characters are quite similar and do not show a clear difference between formal and informal.
- 4–6 marks: Voices of the two characters are different in tone but the formal character is not very formal and does not use sophisticated or specific language.

English 13+ Workbook: Writing by Galore Park

- **7–10 marks:** Voices of the two characters are clearly different in tone and the formal language is sophisticated and precise, and words as well as syntax are formal.

Linking ideas together (page 34)

Try it out

Answers will vary but examples might include:

Linking similar ideas	Linking different ideas
additionally, moreover, furthermore, in addition, similarly, as well as	however, nonetheless, despite, in contrast

Test yourself

Answers will vary.

- **1–3 marks:** A limited number of connectives is used but not consistently or effectively.
- **4–6 marks:** A good range of connectives is used but some may be used repeatedly or inaccurately.
- **7–10 marks:** A range of connectives is used to good effect, acting as signposts to the reader – guiding them through the content of each paragraph and linking the two paragraphs together.

Extend your skills

Answers will vary. Example answer:

The environment is a hot topic currently, as illustrated by the large number of documentaries that have aired on television recently; for example, 'Green Planet', a very popular series which tracks the ongoing destruction of the environment, attracts over 3 million viewers in the UK. Furthermore, its website receives in excess of 800,000 visitors every day, exemplifying just how many people are interested in the plight of our planet. However, just taking an interest is not enough. Making a change is what is needed, specifically a change which is sustained and effective. Looking after the environment is the responsibility of each and every one of us, and in particular young people who are investing in their future. Despite this, many people deny their role in conservation and this must change.

- **1–3 marks:** A limited number of the additional connectives is used but not consistently and not effectively.
- **4–6 marks:** Some of the connectives are used. A range of the additional connectives is used but they may be used repeatedly or inaccurately.
- **7–10 marks:** The full range of connectives is used to good effect, acting as signposts to the reader and guiding them through the content of the paragraph.

Features of non-fiction texts (page 36)

Try it out

Answers will vary. Example answers:

- **Letter** – This is your chance to get involved with after-school sport at …
- **Article** – Sport is more than just keeping fit: every year hundreds of thousands of school students take part in sports clubs and activities beyond their PE lessons.
- **Speech** – Do you like sports? Are you aware of the variety of sporting activities you can access at school and what their benefits are?

Test yourself

Answers will vary.

- **1–3 marks:** Paragraph is a simple summing up. May mention ideas in too much detail. May not use formal language. Speech shows no address to the audience.
- **4–6 marks:** Paragraph concisely sums up the main ideas in a general way. Formal language is used. Quite literal. Addresses the audience using 'you'. Speech shows some or limited reference to the audience.
- **7–10 marks:** Paragraph effectively summarises the key message. Formal language is used in conjunction with comparisons or metaphor to add impact. Addresses the audience directly, perhaps using rhetorical questions. Speech clearly addresses and engages the audience.

Extend your skills

Answers will vary but might include these examples:

Technique	Explanation of its use	Example
Analogy	Comparing two different things with similar aspects	Reading a book is like climbing a ladder; each page is another step.
Hyperbole	Exaggerating for effect	Read this book: it will change your life.
Anaphora	Repeating a word or phrase in successive phrases or sentences	Laughter can be found in books, joy can be found in books, companionship can be found in books.

Planning to inform, explain and advise (page 38)

Try it out

A = advise; E = explain; I = inform

1 E
2 A
3 I
4 A
5 I

Test yourself

Answers will vary. Example plan: How learning has changed in schools during the last 100 years. (see page A6, top)

Extend your skills

Answers will vary. Allow 2 marks for each metaphor:

- **1 mark:** Simple or clichéd comparison used, limited development.
- **2 marks:** Appropriate and original comparison used, developed into a longer phrase or sentence.

Main point	Split main point into smaller reasons/ideas	Fine detail including evidence and statistics
Paragraph 1 – Technology	Use of interactive whiteboards (instead of chalkboards)	Able to use video and pictures in lessons
		Teacher can write on board and save, print or send you the notes
	ICT lessons	Programming is a key skill for life/future jobs
		Helps students who find pen and paper a challenge
Paragraph 2 – Learning outside of the classroom	Trips to museums (instead of relying solely on books)	Help students to understand what life was like in the past
		Art students can see paintings up close to help understand how artists create art
	Forest schools	Benefits of being in nature, such as wellbeing aspects and awareness of the environment
		Learning practical skills
Paragraph 3 – Interactive education	More resources for hands-on lessons	Science equipment – doing experiments is the best way to learn
		Using library resources for research
	Students offered more choice	Opportunity to pursue own interests
		Taking ownership of own learning often makes it more successful

Writing to inform (page 40)

Try it out

Answers will vary. Points should be clearly different from each other.

Test yourself

Answers will vary. Plans should be detailed and show evidence of clearly thought-out points backed up with facts/statistics.

Extend your skills

Answers will vary. The 25 marks available for this question are split as follows:

- Content (/10): Clear and engaging introduction, ideas grouped into paragraphs, detail given including relevant facts/statistics, lively and engaging content, clear conclusion.
- Vocabulary (/5): Formal language, range of sophisticated vocabulary, technical or specific vocabulary used if appropriate.
- Style (/5): Uses a range of connectives, metaphor and/or comparisons, sentence structure is varied.
- Spelling and punctuation (/5): Common spellings and some more complex spellings accurate, punctuation accurate, a wide range of punctuation used (including semi-colons, brackets, dashes, and so on).

Writing about your personal experience (page 42)

Try it out

Answers will vary. Situations noted may be real or imagined.

Test yourself

Answers will vary. The 25 marks available for this question are split as follows:

- Content (/10): Writing is engaging, with interesting detail from personal experience, emotions and reactions are included, close match of topic to task, events are believable, whole piece is focused on the task theme, personal reflection may be included, written in first person and past tense.
- Vocabulary (/5): A range of sophisticated vocabulary which is relevant to the topic, emotive language may be used.
- Style (/5): Uses a range of connectives, literary devices including metaphor and personification, sentence structure is varied for effect.
- Spelling and punctuation (/5): Common spellings and some more complex spellings accurate, punctuation accurate, a wide range of punctuation used (including semi-colons, brackets, dashes, and so on).

Extend your skills

Answers will vary.

Example metaphor: Doing something for the first time – I was the caterpillar, emerging from my chrysalis, learning how to use my wings.

Writing to explain (page 44)

Try it out

Answers will vary.

Example reason with facts and examples: Recycling conserves our natural resources. Every year recycling paper reduces deforestation by 45 per cent. Recycling and reuse of plastic prevents rapid landfill.

Test yourself

Answers will vary. Example explanation: If you could move to any country in the world, where would you choose?

Travel broadens the mind. It has been said that it is the only thing you can buy that makes you happy. In the modern world, commercial travel is easily available and reasonably priced. This opens up the globe to more people, allowing not only holidays but also opportunities to reside in different places. As a result, more and more people are opting to experience life in another corner of the world. There are so many choices of country to relocate to but personally I would choose Japan because the benefits would be abundant.

- 1–3 marks: Simple introduction to the topic. May go into too much detail. Some features of explanation used.
- 4–6 marks: Clear introduction to the topic. A range of features of explanation is used, such as precise vocabulary and 'cause and effect' connectives
- 7–10 marks: Engaging introduction to the topic. A range of features of explanation is used effectively.

Extend your skills

Answers will vary. Up to 3 marks for each metaphor and 1 bonus mark if all three are original and engaging.

- 1 mark if simple or clichéd comparison used, with limited development.
- 2 marks if appropriate and original comparison used, developed into a sentence.
- 3 marks if metaphor links directly to topic, is original and engaging to the reader.

Writing to advise (page 46)

Try it out

Answers will vary. Example advice sentences:

- **Child audience:** Your nearest recycling point is most likely to be at school.
- **Adult audience:** When you do your weekly shopping, think about choosing products with recyclable packaging.

Test yourself

Answers will vary. Plans should include clear pieces of advice, organised into paragraphs, and an engaging introduction and summarising conclusion.

Extend your skills

Answers will vary. The 25 marks available for this question are split as follows:

- Content (/10): Writing is lively and engaging, helpful detail is given, offers a range of different pieces of advice with examples, choice of tone matches audience, personal anecdote may be included, directly addresses the audience, advice is useful and easy to understand.
- Vocabulary (/5): A range of sophisticated vocabulary which is relevant to the topic, language is appropriate to audience.
- Style (/5): Uses a range of connectives, may employ literary devices including metaphor and personification, sentence structure is varied and not overly complex.
- Spelling and punctuation (/5): Common spellings and some more complex spellings accurate, punctuation accurate, a wide range of punctuation used (including semi-colons, brackets, dashes, and so on).

Planning to argue or persuade (page 48)

Try it out

Answers will vary. Examples are given below:

Points in favour	Points against
Technology can make people antisocial.	It helps people to communicate across large distances.
It is a waste of money.	It can make life easier.
It can lead to people losing important skills.	It can be used in education.

Test yourself

Answers will vary. Plans should include a range of arguments on both sides. Examples should be included to support each point in the plan.

Extend your skills

Answers will vary. Example opening sentences:

- **Use of statistics:** At each UK election, over 45 million people vote, but they are all 18 or older.
- **Rhetorical question:** In the globalised society of today, does it really make sense only to experience life in one country?
- **Statement of opinion:** Since the Space Race in the 1950s, considerable amounts of money have been channelled into exploring areas beyond our atmosphere.

Writing to argue (page 50)

Try it out

Answers will vary. The paragraph should outline in detail one specific reason why space travel is a waste of money.

Example point: Too many things to learn about our own planet first, putting people in danger, high spending on only a small number of people, redirect money to charities helping the disadvantaged.

Test yourself

Answers will vary. Plan should show evidence of clear and discrete points in each paragraph, with supporting examples. One clear point of view should be put forward. Counterargument may also be included. Introduction and conclusion should be planned.

Extend your skills

Answers will vary. The 25 marks available for this question are split as follows:

- Content (/10): Writing is lively and appropriate in tone, informative detail is given, a range of different examples are provided, facts and statistics are used to support the argument, expert opinion may be included, discrete points in each paragraph, counterargument is used, introduction and conclusion set out the general viewpoint.
- Vocabulary (/5): A range of sophisticated vocabulary which is relevant to the topic, language is appropriate to audience.
- Style (/5): Uses a range of connectives; may employ literary devices such as metaphor; sentence structure is varied; power of three, assertive style, rhetorical questions and repetition may be used. Writing is cohesive with links made between paragraphs.

- Spelling and punctuation (/5): Common spellings and some more complex spellings accurate, punctuation accurate, a wide range of punctuation used (including semi-colons, brackets, dashes, and so on).

Writing to persuade (page 54)

Try it out

Answers will vary but should include a range of the techniques in the bullet list.

Test yourself

Answers will vary. Plan should show evidence of clear and discrete points in each paragraph, supported by examples. One clear point of view should be put forward. Counterargument may also be included. Introduction and conclusion should be planned.

Extend your skills

Answers will vary. The 25 marks available for this question are split as follows:
- Content (/10): Writing is engaging and appropriate in tone, with interesting detail and a range of different examples provided, facts and statistics are used, expert opinion may be included, discrete points are used in each paragraph, counterargument is used, introduction and conclusion set out the general viewpoint.
- Vocabulary (/5): A range of sophisticated vocabulary which is relevant to the topic, language is appropriate to audience.
- Style (/5): Uses a range of connectives, may employ literary devices such as metaphor; sentence structure is varied; power of three, persuasive phrases, emotive language, assertive style, rhetorical questions and anecdotes may be used.
- Spelling and punctuation (/5): Common spellings and some more complex spellings accurate, punctuation accurate, a wide range of punctuation used (including semi-colons, brackets, dashes, and so on).

Further exam questions (page 58)

Paper 1 Section B: Sample non-fiction writing task response

Write a speech for a school debate either in favour of or against the following statement:

'Technology will ruin our planet'.

In the modern world, technology is omnipresent and omnipotent. We can neither escape its grasp nor fail to be impacted by it in some way. Many people expound the infinite benefits of a world which is increasingly automatic and systematic. However, they fail to see the pitfalls and dangers of a world that is abandoning the human touch.

We only have one planet. Currently, technology is destroying it one charging cable at a time. With all of the new devices and machines that scientists and inventors offer us comes a seemingly innocent charging cable. And what does that charging cable need? Electricity. In the UK, over 80 per cent of our electricity is generated from fossil fuels. Fossil fuels that are rapidly running out. On average, a household owns four smartphones, two tablets and at least two laptops or games consoles. Imagine how much electricity they require to charge! Our addiction to technology is slowly draining the Earth of its natural resources.

Furthermore, the way we use these devices is also detrimental to our world, in particular our relationships and interactions with our fellow humans. We no longer communicate face to face, reading each other's expressions, offering a hand to hold or a shoulder to lean on. We merely send a quick text – sometimes just a 'how r u?', not even bothering to use real words. Our phones are slowly constructing a wall between us and are binding us to our sofas and our bedrooms rather than encouraging us to explore the world outside. Do you want to live in a world where your online friends are your only friends?

Finally, consider how much you yearn for a new iPhone or Xbox. Is it healthy for people to be more concerned by having the latest gadget than about preserving their environment or helping their neighbours? In a world where something new is always on the horizon, we are forgetting to appreciate and value what we already have. We are creating a disposable society where nothing is precious enough to last longer than its new model. If we behave like this towards our possessions, how long will it be until we do the same to our friends and family?

In conclusion, we should be wary of technology in case it further damages our precious world. When you next pick up your phone or laptop, think not only of the electricity that you are wasting or the pollution that is emitted from the power station, but think also of the people who you love and care about and whom you have forsaken in favour of a WhatsApp message or a Snapchat. Remember, those people will be around far longer than the latest software update or faddy app.

Paper 2 Section B: Sample imaginative writing task response

Midnight visitor

The clock strikes midnight and I'm ready. Poised by my windowsill, weapons to hand. Patience is my superpower tonight. When he returns I'll be ready. I was too late last night but now I am the unseen predator, agile and swift in the execution of my will. As I glare out into the unending blackness, I know he's out there and I wonder if he knows that I'm waiting for him, watching him.

Soon, I hear the call of my prey. Far off in the distance, I know he is still out of range. As I raise the eyeglass, I hear him again, taunting me with his whispers. A shadow flashes across my lens but it is fleeting, like a firefly. I wait. Just as I do every night.

My eyelids begin to droop like slack rope but I pinch myself alert again. And I am rewarded. At the edge of my vision, I see him. A smudge of white among the dark forest leaves. A patch in the night sky, growing larger as it approaches. His movements are slow and elegant, like the rising and ebbing tide. His yellow eyes are headlights in the gloom, guiding him through the velvet blackness. His down is soft, ruffling in the wind like furrowed snow. And his wings ... spanning the night sky like an acrobat, as if reaching out for the trapeze, gliding softly through the air as if held by a wire then swooping out of sight, only to return once more, the nocturnal prince of the sky.

As the owl gains on my position, I reach for my artillery. The camera feels like lead in my hands and my fingers like rocks, clumsy and ungainly. Clink. The lens cap tumbles to the floor and I look up, fearful of scaring my visitor away. I shudder as I try to hold the camera still, to capture the perfect shot.

Closer he comes.

Not yet close enough.

Almost.

Now ...

The click of the shutter resonates in my ear and I put down my weapon. Wielding the binoculars once more, I watch as my mark recedes into the shadows, like a hunter inspecting the spoils of victory, and I dare to look at the screen of my camera. There he is. Noble in flight, his eyes fixed on the lens, his wings stretched out as if bowing to the audience. The perfect shot.

Exhausted from the hunt, I climb into bed. The window remains open should my midnight visitor return once more.

Test yourself

Imagine your school has just decided that you will have lessons all day on Sunday, as well as Monday to Friday. Write a brief letter in a formal style to the headteacher, expressing your views on the situation.

_____
_____
_____
_____
_____
_____
_____
_____
_____

Now, using the same points you made in your original letter, write an email in a very informal style to a friend who goes to a different school.

_____
_____
_____
_____
_____
_____
_____ [10 marks]

Extend your skills

Formal language might also be used in narrative writing, for example you might have two very different characters, one formal and the other informal, and you will need to show this in the way they speak.

Write a conversation between a very formal and a very informal character (perhaps a grandparent and grandchild, or an employer and new employee), using their language to tell the reader more about them. Use a separate sheet of paper if necessary.

_____
_____
_____
_____
_____
_____ [10 marks]

Linking ideas together

Connectives, or linking devices, are words and short phrases used to organise a text and guide the reader through the narrative, argument or explanation. They help to join parts of a text together, introduce ideas and signpost for the reader the direction the text is taking. Below are some examples.

Linking similar ideas: furthermore, additionally, therefore

Linking different ideas: conversely, on the other hand, however

It is very important to use these linking words and phrases in essays, articles, reviews, letters and speeches. You may also find yourself using them in comprehension answers. They form the glue that sticks your ideas together and helps the reader to understand what you are trying to express or to follow your line of argument.

They can also order and sequence your ideas. You might even want to include them in your plan.

You should use them:

- at the start of sentences:

> Nonetheless, school uniform remains an important part of students' experiences.

- in the middle of sentences (sometimes after a semi-colon):

> School uniform is compulsory in 99 per cent of institutions but some schools do not require it in Years 12 and 13.

- at the start of paragraphs to indicate how the current paragraph links to the previous one:

> On the other hand, school uniform is a comfort to many students.

Try it out

Using the table below, make a list of as many connectives as you can.

Linking similar ideas	Linking different ideas

➡ Don't overuse connectives. If every sentence contains one, then the writing can become hard to read. Sometimes a simple 'and' or 'but' is enough.

Test yourself

Write two short paragraphs in response to this question:

> Should a uniform be compulsory in all schools?

The first paragraph should give a reason why it ought be compulsory and the second should state why it ought not. Make sure you use connectives to help explain your ideas and to compare the two viewpoints.

_____
_____
_____
_____
_____
_____
_____
_____
_____
_____ [10 marks]

Extend your skills

Other types of connectives are those used for illustrating and emphasising. These will help you to deepen your arguments. Look at the lists below.

Illustrating points	Emphasising points
for example	significantly
as exemplified by	especially
as revealed by	in particular

Write a short but detailed paragraph about the following statement, using some of these and other kinds of linking words and phrases.

> It is everybody's responsibility to look after our environment.

_____
_____
_____
_____
_____ [10 marks]

Features of non-fiction texts

In an exam you are likely to come across a non-fiction writing task. It will probably be an article (usually for a magazine), a speech or a letter. To address the task accurately, you need to be aware of the specific differences between these types of writing.

It is important to consider audience, purpose and tone (APT).

	Audience	Purpose	Tone
Article	Consider who will read the magazine. They will read it at their leisure. The writer is not present when it is read: your writing will need to keep the reader's interest.	This could be to inform, persuade, advise, explain or argue. It is vital to look closely at the wording of the task to identify the purpose.	The style is likely to be formal but may vary depending on the intended audience.
Speech	Your audience is in the room with you. You have direct access to them and they are unlikely to leave. You can address them more directly.		The tone is usually formal but may be different depending on the audience.
Letter	The audience is usually one particular person. They may or may not be someone you know. If you have chosen to write to them, you may already know something of their opinions.		The tone will depend on the audience.

Other points to consider are:

Article:

- Consider your audience, for example a school magazine should be aimed at children; for a specialist interest magazine, you will need plenty of appropriate subject-specific vocabulary.

Speech:

- Address the audience directly using 'you' or 'us' and use questions to make them think.
- Shorter, powerful sentences might be more effective than longer, complex ones.
- Vary the pace by using longer and shorter sentences – hear it as you write it.

Letter:

- Lay out the letter with the address at the top right and the date underneath, and use the correct title for the recipient.
- Always sign off either with 'Yours sincerely' (for recipients whose names you know) or 'Yours faithfully' (for recipients whose names you do not know).
- Tailor what you write to what you know about the recipient. You might use phrases such as 'As you are aware' or 'With the expertise you have, it clear that …'

Try it out

You are going to write about the positive aspects of sport in schools. Write opening sentences for a letter, article and speech on this subject. Think about how they will be different.

_____
_____
_____
_____
_____
_____
_____

Test yourself

Imagine you have been asked to write about the negative impact of technology on young people. Write the final paragraph of an article, and of a speech, on the topic, making sure you consider APT as you write.

_____
_____
_____
_____
_____
_____
_____
_____ [10 marks]

Extend your skills

When writing a speech, there are many techniques, known as rhetorical devices, that can be used for extra impact. Some work for other writing types too. Look on websites about speech writing or in books in the library to find out about three of these techniques. Add these to the table below and then write a short explanation of their use with an example.

Technique	Explanation of its use	Example
Repetition	Using the same words more than once to give emphasis to them	Phones, phones, phones. They're all people seem to care about!

Planning to inform, explain and advise

When writing non-fiction, it is very important to plan. You need to make sure you have enough information and distinct points to avoid becoming repetitive. A similar planning format can be used for the following text types:

Informing: telling somebody about a topic, including many aspects of the topic (this is not the same as persuading or arguing), for example:

> Write an article for a school magazine about healthy eating.

Explaining: detailing a process or giving a detailed definition or description of what something is and how it works, for example:

> Write a letter to an alien, explaining to them what the internet is.

Advising: giving somebody guidance or recommendations on a topic, for example:

> Write a letter to your six-year-old self, giving advice on what the next six years at school will be like and how to make the most of them.

The planning format looks like this:

Introduction   Point → Evidence → Explanation
Paragraph 2   Point → Evidence → Explanation
Paragraph 3   Point → Evidence → Explanation
(Depending on the time you have, you may cover more points than this)
Conclusion

Make sure each paragraph has a clear and distinct point and purpose.

Try it out

Look at the following tasks. Decide whether they are advising, explaining or informing by writing A, E or I in the space next to each one.

1. Your headteacher has decided to get rid of school lunches and everyone will have to bring a lunch from home. Write a letter to him or her outlining your views on the topic. _____

2. Imagine your brother or sister is joining your school as you leave. Write a short speech to deliver to them about how to survive, thrive and make friends. _____

3. Write a blog article about your favourite author. _____

4. Write an article for a school magazine about how to become widely read. _____

5. Write an essay about how learning has changed in schools during the last 100 years. _____

> → Regularly read newspapers, blogs and magazines and watch the news to keep up to date and well-informed on current issues. You will find a list of some of the most common topics for exam questions in the **Further exam questions** section on page 58.

Test yourself

Use the planning format below to plan one of the tasks from the **Try it out** section opposite.

Main point	Split main point into smaller reasons/ ideas	Fine detail including evidence and statistics
Paragraph 1		
Paragraph 2		
Paragraph 3		

Extend your skills

To make this type of writing really engaging for the reader, you could introduce figurative language. You might even begin to develop this at the planning stage. Try creating a simile or metaphor for each of the five tasks in the list on the page opposite, for example:

> **2** Starting school is like standing at the foot of a mountain – you'll reach the top with hard work and determination!

_____
_____
_____
_____
_____
_____
_____
_____ [10 marks]

Planning to inform, explain and advise

Writing to inform

Writing to inform means providing the reader with information that is impartial (not giving any particular opinion or bias) and accurate. You are not trying to convince or persuade the reader.

These are examples of questions that require you to write to inform:

> - Write an article for your school magazine about great things to do over the summer holidays in your local area.
> - Write an article to be placed in a time capsule, telling future students of your school about what it is like now.
> - Write a letter to a student who is going to join your school, telling them what you think they should know before they join.

Informative writing:

- includes many facts that are relevant to the topic
- presents a balanced view
- is clear and sounds authoritative
- is written formally
- uses analogy and description to help the reader understand facts
- uses connectives and conjunctions to guide the reader through the text.

Here is an example:

> The Lake District offers extensive opportunities for outdoor pursuits. The challenging peaks are enjoyed by tens of thousands of hikers every year. For me, the view from the summit is always worth the climb. Moreover, from the top of Scafell Pike, you can see Derwent Water, stretching out below you like a blue-tinted mirror, peppered with the white sails of small boats and the bright colours of kayaks. Water-based activities are also a thrilling aspect of a holiday in the Lakes.

Try it out

Choose one of the tasks in the green box above and make a list of the main points you would make. An example is provided:

Impressions of Thailand

1. How you travelled to Thailand
2. The city of Bangkok
3. Exploring the beaches
4. Visiting temples
5. The food

Your task: _____

1. _____
2. _____
3. _____
4. _____
5. _____

→ Always try to choose a topic that you know in depth and feel confident about. Your writing will then sound more knowledgeable.

Test yourself

Plan one of the following tasks:

- Write a letter to the governors of your school, telling them about the changes you and your classmates would like to make to the school.
- Write an essay about how you think the world will be different in 25 years' time.
- Write an article for your school magazine about the extra-curricular activities available at the school.

Extend your skills

On a separate sheet of paper, write up in full the piece you planned in **Test yourself** above.

[25 marks]

Writing about your personal experience

Some questions in the 'Writing to inform' category require you to write about your own experience, for example:

- Write about a time when you had to stand up for yourself or someone else.
- Write about a time when you learnt a valuable lesson.
- Write about a person who you find inspirational.

In some ways, these are easy tasks because you are writing about something you know a lot about – yourself! However, there are some common pitfalls:

- As you experienced these things, it is easy to forget to add interesting facts or explain the situation in sufficient detail.
- When writing about yourself, it can be easy to fall into the trap of starting every sentence with 'I'.
- As the writing feels quite factual, it is easy to omit imagery and engaging vocabulary to bring the story to life.

This example from a response to the 'valuable lesson' question above shows how to avoid these pitfalls:

I knew he was wrong. I knew the rumours weren't true. I knew I had to do something but there was a niggling feeling inside me, stopping me from saying anything, clamping my lips shut like a cell door. With an uneasy feeling lingering in my gut, I walked away but the episode was branded on my mind. Nobody deserved to be treated that way. Nobody deserved to be made to feel so small. Nobody deserved to spend their school days feeling fearful and ashamed.

Notice that the repetition of 'I knew' is fine when used deliberately for emphasis, like this. However, also note that none of the other sentences begin with 'I'.

Try it out

Make a note below of a time, real or imagined, when:

You did something for the first time	
Something or someone surprised you	
You were embarrassed	
You felt afraid	
You visited a memorable place	

Test yourself

Choose one of your scenarios from **Try it out** and write three paragraphs about it. Remember to avoid the pitfalls outlined opposite.

_____
_____
_____
_____
_____
_____
_____
_____
_____
_____
_____
_____
_____
_____
_____
_____
_____
_____ [25 marks]

→ You don't always have to write about your own experience. It is fine to invent it instead, as long as it is believable. Your aim is to inform the reader in an engaging fashion – a little exaggeration or added detail may help you to achieve that purpose.

Extend your skills

Create a metaphor or simile that sums up the whole situation you are writing about, for example having to stand up to somebody powerful might be 'like standing at a crossroads without a map to show you the best route'.

_____
_____
_____
_____

Writing to explain

When you write to explain, you are outlining or detailing a process for the reader. You might be writing about how something works or happens, providing reasons for this and answers to potential questions.

Explanatory writing:

- is clear and succinct
- gives reasons for things – explains why and how
- uses relevant or technical vocabulary
- uses connectives to help the reader navigate their way through your ideas and understand the cause and effect of a process
- occasionally uses metaphor to help engage the reader.

Read this example question:

> Write an article for your school magazine about the importance of recycling.

Consider this structure:

Introduction
- Explain the main idea of the topic, for example: Recycling is becoming more and more crucial as the world's natural resources become depleted.

Each main paragraph
- Provide a clear reason with examples and an explanation, for example: Recycling paper is important because too many trees are being felled to make more paper products. Trees are important to the environment as they produce oxygen. In 2016 the size of the Amazon rainforest decreased by over 15 per cent.
- Use statistics and facts, like the ones above, to engage the reader. When you are writing in the exam, you can invent these if you need to, as long as they sound believable.
- Sound authoritative, for example use 'it is known that' rather than 'some people believe'.

Conclusion
- Recap your main reasons and refer back to the main idea of the explanation.

Other things to consider:

- Ensure you sound truthful by choosing reasons carefully and giving detail.
- Appeal to the reader or listener by using 'you' and speaking to them directly. Use questions to engage them with your ideas.
- Think about each reason you have given in your argument and think about the opposite opinion. Try to address this in your writing and explain how the opposite opinion is not correct.

> ➡ Make sure you explain why things happen and what their effect is, using connectives such as because, due to, therefore, consequently, leads to and caused by.

Try it out

List reasons why recycling is important. Then add a fact or example to support each reason.

_____

_____

_____

Test yourself

Look at these three explanation questions. Choose one and write the opening paragraph, outlining the main idea of the topic without going into all of the individual reasons.

- If you could move to any country in the world, where would you choose? Write an essay explaining your choice.
- What do you think makes a good friend? Explain your ideas in an article for a school website.
- Write a letter to a new student at your school explaining what life is like in Years 7 and 8.

_____
_____
_____
_____
_____
_____
_____
_____
_____ [10 marks]

Extend your skills

To engage the reader, you will need to use language to create particular effects. This may include using metaphor. Create a metaphor to use in each of the tasks above, for example for the 'good friend' article:

> A truly good friend is like an acrobat's safety net – you know they're there to catch you, even when you don't need them to.

_____
_____
_____
_____
_____
_____
_____
_____
_____ [10 marks]

Writing to advise

Writing to advise involves giving suggestions or help to somebody, often based on your own experience. Advice questions look like this:

> - Write a letter to a friend who is struggling with their exams, giving them advice on how to cope with the pressure and organise their revision.
> - Write an article for a local newspaper about how to keep healthy.
> - Write a speech to deliver in assembly about how to be a good friend.

Different audiences usually require different content and tone, for example imagine you are writing about keeping healthy …

- to a ten-year-old:

> Make the most of school PE lessons and when you find a sport you really enjoy, try to find an after-school club so that you can keep more active doing something you like.

- to an adult:

> A good way to fit exercise into a busy life is to make it part of your journey to work. Walk, run or cycle to the office and you will not only keep fit and healthy but also feel energised for your day.

When writing to advise, try to put yourself in your audience's shoes. Consider:

- What do they need advice about and why?
- What do they already know on the topic?
- What have you experienced or have knowledge of that might help them?

> → Anecdotes, or personal stories, are useful when writing to advise but keep them short, engaging and relevant. They can be a good way to spark or maintain the reader's interest.

Try it out

Look at the task below and write two sentences that you could use in your answer – one aimed at an adult and one aimed at a child.

> Write an article about how to live an environmentally friendly life.
>
> You might refer to:
> - recycling
> - using public transport
> - energy-saving methods or devices.

_____

_____

_____

_____

Test yourself

Choose one of the three tasks from the page opposite and plan it.

____

Extend your skills

Write up the piece in full that you planned in **Test yourself** above. You may need to continue on a separate sheet of paper.

____

[25 marks]

Planning to argue or persuade

When you are asked to argue or persuade in your writing, you will choose one side of an issue or question. However, when planning for this, you need to consider both sides of the argument because you can benefit by addressing some counterarguments and then dismissing them.

Look at the following planning template, which has been completed to answer this question:

> 'School uniform should be compulsory in every school.' Write a speech either agreeing or disagreeing with this statement.

Introduction: A clear statement of the topic and the main viewpoint.

Pros/In favour/Advantages	Cons/Against/Disadvantages
School uniform makes everyone equal.	All wearing the same thing is not fair as some people will feel uncomfortable.
School uniform looks smart.	Being comfortable is more important for good learning.
Uniform takes the stress out of getting ready in the morning.	Choosing your clothes is part of your individuality. It's not reflective of real life to all dress the same.
Uniforms make us feel part of a community.	By all looking the same, students may be compared more directly to those around them, causing self-esteem issues.

Conclusion: A summing up of key points and restatement of the viewpoint.

If you were agreeing with the statement about school uniform, you might write:

> School uniform is a vital part of school life as it provides a level playing field for all. Nobody has to worry about having the latest fashions and it leads to a reduction in arguments or jealousies. Some might say that this is not reflective of real life but, at such a young age, this isn't a relevant factor. Students are learning to be tolerant and self-confident and uniform can help them to do this.

If you were disagreeing, you would use the right-hand side of the table for your main points and the left-hand side as your counterargument.

> → When planning out your ideas, don't forget to consider how your essay will end. The final sentence can have a powerful effect on the reader and is worth planning from the outset.

Try it out

Look at this task and write down three points in favour of the statement and three points against it.

> Technology is detrimental to society.

Points in favour	Points against

Test yourself

Use the planning template to plan one of the tasks below:

- In preparation for a debate, write a speech either for or against the statement 'Children should be able to vote from the age of 16'.
- Write a persuasive letter to your parents convincing them to move to a country of your choice.
- Write an article for a magazine with the title 'Space travel is a waste of money'.

Introduction:	
Pros/In favour/Advantages	Cons/Against/Disadvantages
Conclusion:	

For each 'In favour' or 'Against' argument you add to the plan, offer a detail or an example to support it.

Extend your skills

The opening sentence of your essay is very important. You could choose for your starting point:

- an anecdote, quotation or statistic
- a rhetorical question
- a statement of opinion.

Select one of the tasks from **Test yourself** and, on a separate sheet of paper, write one of each type of opening sentence for it.

Planning to argue or persuade

Writing to argue

When you write to argue, it is often in preparation for a debate, and you may be given the choice as to whether you argue 'for' or 'against' a statement, for example:

> Write a debate speech either for or against this statement: 'This house believes that space travel is a waste of money.'

The purpose of an argument text is to influence the reader's ideas or opinions.

There are several things you need to do to write a clear argument:

- Present your overall point of view in the introductory paragraph.
- Use the first sentence of each paragraph to introduce its topic.
- Introduce counterarguments. Depending on the task, you may:
  - discuss their merits
  - try to show how they are incorrect.
- Be assertive – 'I know' is stronger than 'I think'.
- Use connectives to signpost your argument for the reader.
- Be rational – readers appreciate reasons and logic in an argument.
- Use formal language (unless the question asks you to be lighthearted or tells you that the audience is your peers).

Here is an example of an introduction to the debate speech:

> Look at it go. Billions of dollars of money, burning away at the base of a rocket. Going up in flames. What a waste! It is a fact that space travel is an enormous waste of money. It is dangerous, damaging to the environment and utterly pointless. Clearly our focus should be on improving our own planet rather than expending valuable resources exploring other planets for no good reason. We should be spending that money more wisely.

→ When you are arguing a point, it is important to use the language of argument effectively. Use groups of three ideas or adjectives to emphasise a key point, use facts and figures to support your ideas and use repetition to make your point memorable to the reader.

Try it out

Write the next paragraph of the speech above. What will be its main topic?

_____

_____

_____

_____

_____

Test yourself

Choose one of the following tasks and create a plan for it using the template below.

- Your local council has announced that it might have to close your nearest park. Write a letter to them arguing either for or against its closure.
- Write a debate speech either 'for' or 'against' this statement: 'This house believes that advertising for sugary foods should be banned from all television channels.'
- Write an article with the title 'Are computers ruining our lives?'

Introduction:	
Pros/In favour/Advantages	**Cons/Against/Disadvantages**
Conclusion:	

→ For each point in your argument, offer an example or facts and statistics to support it.

Extend your skills

Now write your speech in full below using the advice in the bullets on page 50 to help you.

[25 marks]

Writing to persuade

When you write to persuade, you are trying to convince the reader to believe or do something. We most commonly see persuasive writing in advertisements and during political debates. On a more day-to-day basis you may find yourself persuading a parent or guardian to let you go on a trip or to buy you a treat.

To be convincingly persuasive, you need to do the following:

- Focus on your side of the issue.
  - Counterarguments should only be used if you can show why they are incorrect.
- Be assertive – if you sound confident you will be more convincing.
  - For example: I am sure … These facts and figures are indisputable …
- Repeat words or ideas to help them embed.
- Use the power of three – groups of three words or ideas, which will stand out to a reader.
- Use persuasive phrases to start your paragraphs and sentences.
  - For example: It is evident that … Clearly …
- Use rhetorical questions to make the reader stop and think.
  - For example: Didn't you enjoy treating yourself when you were a teenager?
- Play on your audience's emotions – make them feel something.
  - Use emotive language to do this, for example: I will be an outcast in the playground, isolated from my peers and shunned if I am not allowed to go to the Snow Dome.
- Use 'we' and 'us' to draw the reader into your argument.
  - For example: Together, we can reach a mutually acceptable solution.

Try it out

Write a short speech to your parent or guardian, persuading them to let you go to a party or event that they are not keen for you to attend.

_____
_____
_____
_____
_____
_____
_____
_____

> → When being persuasive, knowledge of your audience is your most valuable weapon. What would be persuasive to a 12-year-old might not be so convincing to an adult.

Test yourself

Choose and plan an answer to one of the following questions:

- An opportunity has arisen at school for one student to gain some work experience at a high-profile company. Write a letter to the headteacher persuading him or her that you are the best candidate for the programme.
- Write a speech, to be delivered to your family, persuading them to relocate to a country of your choice.
- Write a letter to your local MP persuading him or her to improve recycling facilities in your area.

Extend your skills

Now write your response in full below, using the advice in the bullets on page 54 to help you.

[25 marks]

Example exam questions

Below you will find some example exam questions from the writing parts of the Common Entrance at 13+ exam.

Try it out

Read them carefully and make some notes about which you would choose and what you would write about.

Test yourself

Create plans for the tasks that you would choose to complete. This could be part of your revision timetable as the exam gets closer. Try writing some of the plans in the time you will be allowed in the exam – around 5 minutes is the average planning time in a 13+ exam.

Paper 1 Section B – Non-fiction writing task

Each task is worth 25 marks. Credit will be given for good spelling and punctuation and appropriate presentation, as well as for a range of appropriate vocabulary. The questions in this section fall into a range of non-fiction genres. Read each question carefully to work out whether it is an informing, explaining, persuading, arguing or advising task. It may also be a question on an aspect of a literature text.

- 'Youth is wasted on the young.'

    Write an article for a school magazine explaining the benefits of being young.

- Write a speech for a school debate either in favour of or against the following statement:

    'Technology will ruin our planet.'

- Your local council has decided to close all of the leisure centres in your area.

    Write a letter to your local councillor, persuading them to keep the centres open.

- You have received a letter from an alien asking you to explain what 'art' is. Write your reply.

- Write a speech to deliver to your class about your favourite hobby. Tell them what your hobby is, what it entails, the benefits of the hobby and what you learn from it.

- EITHER

    Write about a text that shocked you.

    Refer to at least two episodes in the text which were shocking and explain why they had this effect on you and how the author achieved this.

    OR

    Write about a text that helped you to learn about a particular issue or problem that other people might face.

    Explain how it improved your understanding of the topic and the effect it had on you while you were reading it and since then.

Extend your skills

Think about the different types of writing task and consider other topics that might come up in an exam. Write your own questions in the exam style.

Paper 2 Section B – Imaginative writing

Each task is worth 25 marks. Credit will be given for good spelling and punctuation and appropriate presentation, as well as for imaginative and exciting use of vocabulary. Questions in this section fall into either the description or narrative genre. If not explicitly stated, you can choose which one to use.

- Write a story using **one** of the following titles:
  - Liar liar
  - Far, far away
  - The headache
  - Dark skies
  - The siren
- Write a description of the sights, sounds and atmosphere in a busy market.
- Earthquake!
- Write a story that includes the words 'And then it was gone …'
- Write about a time when you had to ask for help. You might like to include:
  - why you had to ask for help
  - who you asked and why you chose them
  - how their help affected you
  - how you felt asking for help.
- Write about a time when you felt embarrassed.
- Write a story that begins or ends with the words 'Our troubles were only just beginning.'
- Midnight visitor
- Write about a time when you had to make a difficult decision.
- Broken promises

You will find a sample response for one non-fiction writing task and one imaginative writing task in the Answers section.

Topics to be aware of and explore

In Paper 1, Section B you will be asked to write about something factual, rather than imaginary. To do this, you need not only to show writing skill, but also some knowledge about the topic you are asked to write about.

Try it out

Below are some common topics that come up in the exam. Read through them, look at the prompt questions and make some notes for each one.

Extend your skills

You could also conduct some research on the topics you are less familiar with by looking at news articles to find out what is currently happening within these areas. Referring to topical events will look good in your writing.

Sport
- What are its benefits?
- Should it be compulsory in schools?
- What are the downfalls of professional sports?

_____
_____
_____
_____
_____
_____
_____
_____
_____
_____
_____
_____
_____
_____

Technology
- What are its advantages/disadvantages?
- Where is technology heading in the future?
- Are there any developments that have been detrimental?
- Is the cost of technology too high?
- Is space travel worth pursuing?

_____
_____
_____
_____
_____
_____
_____
_____
_____

School life
- Should we wear uniform?
- How could the curriculum be different?
- Are school hours and holidays too long or short?
- What are the benefits of extra-curricular activities?

_____
_____
_____
_____
_____
_____
_____
_____

Topics to be aware of and explore

Environment
- Whose responsibility is it to look after our world?
- What is the future of our world?
- How can we protect the environment?
- Can one person make a difference?
- How is the environment protected in your local area/school?

_____
_____
_____
_____
_____
_____
_____
_____
_____

Charity
- Why should we give to charity?
- Do some charities deserve more support than others?
- Which charities do you know about?
- In what ways can we support charities?

_____
_____
_____
_____
_____
_____
_____
_____

Education
- What advice would you give to people starting school?
- Should education be free?
- At what age should you start or finish school?

_____
_____
_____
_____
_____
_____
_____
_____
_____

Politics
- At what age should young people be able to vote?
- Is politics relevant to young people?
- On what topics should the government consult with young people?

_____
_____
_____
_____
_____
_____
_____
_____
_____

Topics to be aware of and explore

Growing up
- What are the challenges of growing up?
- What would you advise your younger self now you have the benefit of hindsight?
- Which age have you most enjoyed being?
- What are you looking forward to about being older or going to secondary school?
- What would you like to do as a career?

_____
_____
_____
_____
_____
_____
_____
_____

Ethics
- Is it always wrong to lie?
- Should all secrets be kept secret?
- What makes a good friend?
- Is it sometimes good to make a mistake?
- What is the difference between being lonely and being alone?
- Is violence ever the answer?

_____
_____
_____
_____
_____
_____
_____
_____

Topics to be aware of and explore